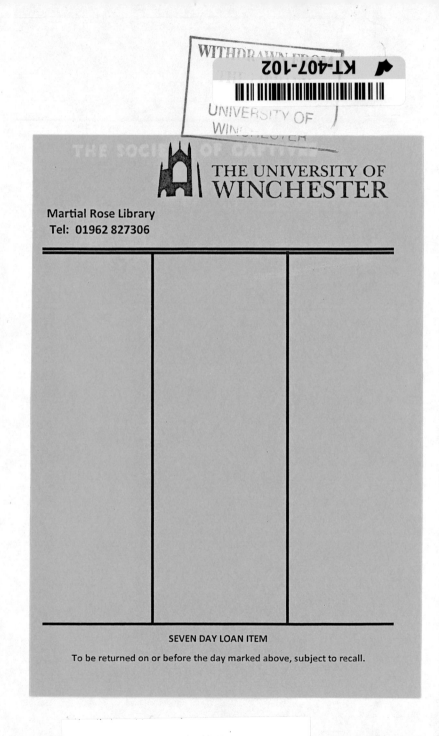

PRINCETON UNIVERSITY PRESS

PRINCETON AND OXFORD

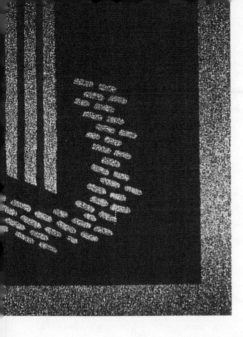

THE SOCIETY OF CAPTIVES

A STUDY OF A

MAXIMUM SECURITY PRISON

BY GRESHAM M. SYKES

With a new introduction by
Bruce Western and a new
epilogue by the author

First edition, 1958
First Princeton Classic Edition, with a new introduction by Bruce
Western and a new epilogue by the author, 2007

Portions of the discussion concerning the corruption of the guard's
authority are from *Crime and Society*, by Gresham M. Sykes.
Copyright 1956 by Random House, Inc. Reprinted by permission
of Random House, Inc.

The material in the epilogue has been reprinted from *Punishment
and Social Control*, 2d ed., Blomberg and Cohen, eds., pp.
357–365. Copyright © 2003 Walter de Gruyter, Inc. Published by
Aldine de Gruyter, Hawthorne, New York.

Library of Congress Cataloging-in-Publication Data

Sykes, Gresham M.
    The society of captives : a study of a maximum security prison /
by Gresham M. Sykes ; with a new introduction by Bruce Western and a new epilogue by the author. — 1st Princeton classic ed.
        p. cm. — (Princeton classic editions)
    Originally published, 1958.
    Includes bibliographical references.
    ISBN-13: 978-0-691-13064-4 (pb : alk. paper)
    ISBN-10: 0-691-13064-7 (pb : alk. paper)
    1. State Prison, Trenton (N.J.) 2. Prisons—New Jersey—
Case studies. 3. Prison administration—New Jersey—History.
4. Prisoners—New Jersey—Case studies. I. Title.
    HV9475.N52T77 2007
    65'.33—dc23   2006052590

British Library Cataloging-in-Publication Data is available

Printed on acid-free paper. ∞

press.princeton.edu

Printed in the United States of America

10 9 8 7 6

THIS BOOK IS DEDICATED TO THE MAN IN PRISON—

BOTH THE PRISONER AND HIS GUARD

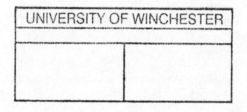

CONTENTS

INTRODUCTION TO THE
PRINCETON CLASSIC EDITION
BY BRUCE WESTERN

IN THE SUMMER of 2003 I taught an undergraduate criminology class to a group of prisoners at New Jersey State Prison—the site of Gresham Sykes's *Society of Captives*. The obvious relevance of the case study, its beautiful writing, and classic status all made *Captives* essential reading. The book provoked a lively discussion. Sykes's survey of the pains of imprisonment resonated with the students' experience of incarceration. But they were unconvinced that the guards lacked total power as Sykes had claimed. From the students' perspective, official control was far-reaching indeed. At a deeper level, the class exemplified a key thesis of the book. Organized by the prisoners themselves, the class disrupted boredom and contributed in a small way to the order of prison life. Just as Sykes found five decades earlier, leaders among the prisoners were helping to sustain order in the inmate society.

Sykes's work captured basic truths about penal confinement, and the field research still rings true. Yet the penal system has changed fundamentally. By the end of the 1990s, a young black man in America was more likely to have a prison record than a bachelor's degree. And if he had dropped out of high school, he had a better than even chance of going to prison before turning forty. Poor young men—especially African American men—now confront the power of

I thank Gresham Sykes for his gracious advice and assistance. Devah Pager provided helpful comments on an earlier draft. Alice Goffman also provided invaluable comments and research assistance.

the state in the person of the policeman, the parole officer, and the prison guard. When Sykes began his research in 1954, America's prison population was just one-eighth as large as it would be fifty years later. The penal system had not yet gained a central place in American race relations and urban poverty. Still, *The Society of Captives* remains a cornerstone of prison sociology and indispensable for those who would understand the current era of mass incarceration.

These days, we tend to look in free society for the prison's significance. We study the prison's effects on crime rates, or poverty, or family life. Sykes draws us back inside the institution, delving into the internal logic of the prison society. There, he finds that the legitimate use of force by prison officials is an inadequate source of social order. Order, he shows, is produced by a social struggle within prison walls that today is conducted on a greatly enlarged scale. While Sykes redirects our attention to the conditions of penal confinement, he also provides a vivid metaphor for what the ghetto has become. Just as the prison has a burgeoning role in the lives of America's urban poor, so too do a variety of social control agencies. In this context, *Captives* remains invaluable not just for its focus on a correctional facility but for its analysis of a society suffused by official supervision.

Inmate Society and the Limits of Repression

In *The Society of Captives* Sykes identifies, and then resolves, a two-part problem of social order. First, social order is tenuous in captive societies like the prison. Although they recognize the authority of the custodians, the inmates do not feel bound by a moral duty to obey. "In the prison," writes Sykes, "power must be based on something other than internalized morality and the custodians find themselves confronting men who must be forced, bribed, or cajoled into compliance."[1] Second, the vast repressive power of

---

[1] *The Society of Captives*, hereafter *SOC*, p. 47.

authorities is inefficient for maintaining order. Besides penal discipline, the everyday tasks of the total institution include cooking, cleaning, and rehabilitation as well. These tasks require at least a little independence. As Sykes observes, "[T]he ability of the officials to physically coerce their captives into the paths of compliance is something of an illusion as far as the day-to-day activities of the prison are concerned."[2] The stunted moral authority of the guards combined with the limited efficacy of official violence yield what Sykes memorably describes as the "defects of total power."

The total power of the guards is defective, but penal harm—"the pains of imprisonment"—remains extensive.[3] Although it has discarded corporal punishment and is reasonably habitable, the modern prison corrodes the inmate's person and sense of moral worth. By losing his freedom, the inmate surrenders the powers that define citizenship in a liberal society.[4] Deprived of nearly all personal possessions, the inmate also forfeits the markers of biography and individuality. The prisoner loses autonomy as well as individuality because movement and routine are minutely controlled. Regimented line movements, regular head counts, bans on gambling, and dozens of other rules of maximum custody seem unaccountable and gratuitous to the inmates. Prisoners are not just assailed by carceral supervision; threats to personal safety from other inmates make prison life unpredictable. At times these threats take a sexual form. The weak are raped and sometimes recruited into sexual service. The pains of imprisonment can thus extend beyond the inmate's physical identity to his gender identity too. Sykes's inventory of the pains of imprisonment closes with a potent existential appraisal:

[H]owever painful these frustrations or deprivations may be in the immediate terms of thwarted goals, discomfort, boredom, and lone-

---

[2] Ibid., p. 49.
[3] Ibid., chapter 4.
[4] In this introduction I refer to prisoners as men. Over 90 percent of prison inmates in the United States are men, but more importantly, pris-

liness, they carry a more profound hurt as a set of threats or attacks which are directed against the very foundations of the prisoner's being. The individual's picture of himself as a person of value—as a morally acceptable, adult male who can present some claim to merit in his material achievements and his inner strength—begins to waver and grow dim.[5]

The pains of imprisonment form the uneven bedrock on which the social order of the prison must be built. Each character in the inmate social structure—revealed by the local argot—responds differently. For the *rats* and the *center men*, the pains of imprisonment are relieved by betraying other inmates and siding with prison officials. The *gorillas* and *merchants* exploit their fellow inmates either through violence or commerce in contraband. The sexually predatory *wolf*, the rebellious *ball buster* and the impulsively violent *tough* all add to the volatility of prison life. But those who trade in violence retain a little masculinity, and thus some personal vitality, in a society of strict control.

Social cohesion among the prisoners is fostered by the *real man*. The real man embodies values of manhood and integrity. Self-controlled, taciturn, and aloof, the real men of New Jersey State Prison show fortitude by "pulling their own time." The real man, Sykes writes, recovers his integrity in the face of severe privation, "for the real man regains his autonomy, in a sense, by denying the custodians' power to strip him of his ability to control himself."[6] The dignified endurance of the real man exemplifies inmate decorum. Respected by all, the real man stifles conflict with the guards and builds cohesion among inmates.

In their wide discretion to apply force and enforce rules, guards also play a crucial role in keeping the peace. Guards in an orderly unit seek out the real men to make small

---

ons are deeply gendered institutions, and much of Sykes's analysis stems from his focus on a men's facility.

[5] *SOC*, p. 79.
[6] Ibid., p. 102.

trades, turning a blind eye to minor disobedience to secure cooperation in other areas. This petty corruption originates in the structure of the captive society, where there are few rewards in the everyday routines of the prisoners. For order to prevail, guards must moderate their reliance on coercion and inmates must actively cooperate in their own incarceration.

The balance between guard and inmate can certainly be found in the captive society, but Sykes shows that it is inherently unstable. In the years before he visited New Jersey State Prison, riots had disrupted the daily routine. Hostages were taken and property was damaged. The riots, says Sykes, were a response to a repressive phase in prison management. Escalating repression was itself an effort to reverse the lax discipline of the previous decade. The tightening up of prison routines severely reduced the informal power of the inmates, who rebelled in return. As Sykes observed, "The effort of the custodians to 'tighten up' the prison undermines the cohesive forces at work in the inmate population and it is these forces which play a critical part in keeping the society of the prison on an even keel."[7] Prison officials clamped down on the inmates' informal social order, jeopardizing the leadership of the real men, who eschewed conflict and violence. The gorillas and toughs seized the reins, and order succumbed to chaos. The analysis of acute conflict provides the clearest evidence for Sykes's theory of social order: conflict was controlled not by official repression but by the active cooperation of those prisoners oriented to social cohesion. The informal order of the prisoners was temporary, however. Inmate self-governance threatened the control of authorities, so periods of order sometimes gave way to increased discipline and riotous reaction.

In one hundred and thirty short pages, Sykes provided a penetrating and wide-ranging analysis of the captive soci-

[7] Ibid., p. 124.

ety. Later studies would either view the prison from below, as a criminological problem, or from above, as a problem in public administration.[8] *Captives* remains original by seeking the sources of prison society in the perspectives of guards and inmates, and the interaction between them. These interactions reveal Sykes's prison as a negative space consisting of refusal and denial, in which carceral pain is everywhere, in which privileges can be lost, but few rewards are earned. In this setting, social order is fragile, sustained by petty corruption that must remain hidden from free society and official acknowledgement.

This analysis of the prison social system fast became a classic work. Sykes was plain-spoken, rejecting the obscure language that clouded postwar sociology. His elegant prose examined the informal basis of the prison's social order, the internal stratification of inmate society, and the precarious balance between guards and inmates—themes that echoed through prison field studies in the decades after *Captives* was published.[9] Not just emulated, the book also set the terms of key debates about the links between society and the prison and the role of prison officials in the maintenance of order.

Society and the Guards: Two Debates over *Captives*

Captives stimulated two debates that remain important as we try to understand the great changes in the American penal system over the last thirty years. Some writers charged that the prison was substantially a product of the society in which it was embedded and not the autonomous social system that Sykes described. Others claimed that the

---

[8] John Irwin's *The Felon* (Englewood Cliffs, NJ: Prentice-Hall, 1970) exemplifies the criminological approach. John DiIulio's *Governing Prisons* (New York: Free Press, 1987) takes the public administration perspective.

[9] The classic status of *Captives* is discussed by Jonathan Simon, "The 'Society of Captives' in the Era of Hyper-Incarceration," *Theoretical Criminology*, Vol. 4, 2000, pp. 285–308, and Michael Reisig, "The Champion, Contender, and Challenger: Top-Ranked Books in Prison Studies," *Prison Journal*, Vol. 81, 2001, pp. 389–407.

disciplinary role of prison staff and managers is far more central than Sykes suggested.

Sykes's prison is in many ways a self-contained social system. The book's title conveys a world operating within prison walls, a "society" following its own tempo and dynamics. In the first few pages, the prison is offered as a microcosm, a "small-scale society," which can offer deeper understanding of racial divisions, employment, and ultimately totalitarianism.[10] The powerful internal dynamic grows from the pains of imprisonment. The roles that inmates adopted and the relations between guards and inmates were responses to systemic discomforts and deprivations.

Sykes's emphasis on the internal sources of prison society contrasts with the view of prison shaped by the social forces of free society. In *The Prison Community* (1940), the forerunner to *Captives* published eighteen years earlier, Donald Clemmer argued that the prison's social hierarchy reflected the social status of inmates before their incarceration. Clemmer's field observation and survey analysis of a midwestern prison revealed three rough groups: an elite, a middle class, and a lower class of "hoosiers," whose inferiority left them barely aware of their collective identity. These groups were less distinct, Clemmer argued, than in free society where social interaction promoted group cohesion.[11] Twelve years after the publication of *Captives*, John Irwin, writing *The Felon* (1970), also saw the inmate's status before incarceration as affecting his place in the prison pecking order. Whereas Clemmer appealed to social class, Irwin related the inmate's identity and behavior to his membership in a criminal subculture. The felon's incarceration is just one stage in a lifetime of deviance, and the subculture prepares him for prison time.[12] Just as the felon is rooted in

---

[10] *SOC*, p. xxxii.
[11] Donald Clemmer, *The Prison Community*, 1940; reprint, New York: Rinehart, 1958, pp. 107–109.
[12] *The Felon*, p. 63.

his subculture, so too does Irwin's prison inherit the opposi-
tional norms and social solidarities of the subculture of career criminals.

Several years later, James Jacobs's *Stateville* (1977)
added to the list of societal influences on the prison by fo-
cusing on the prison managers. Jacobs described how Stateville Penitentiary in Illinois coped with the expansion of rehabilitative programming as technocracy burgeoned in
society as a whole in the decade after World War II. The authoritarian regime of Stateville crumbled through the
1960s, as institutional power was challenged inside the facility and out. Jacobs's analysis shifts attention from the inmate social structure to the historical and institutional influences on prison administration.[13]

By emphasizing regimes of prison administration, Jacobs
foreshadowed a second debate, over the influence of staff
and managers on the quality of prison life. John DiIulio in
Governing Prisons (1987) forcefully challenged the project
of prison sociology by arguing for the decisive impact of
prison officials—not inmates—on the quality of prison life.
In a jab, not just at Sykes but at Irwin and Jacobs too, Di-
Iulio argued that prison officials are the government behind
the walls and "are neither the pawns of inmate society nor
captives of broader sociopolitical developments."[14] DiIulio
claimed that the quality of prison life would improve with a
bureaucratized, paramilitary style of prison management
which maintains order through strict control. Tough discipline of this bureaucratized kind would not only preserve
order, but promote rehabilitation too. DiIulio's penal discipline relies little on trust in inmates or their capacity for cooperation or self-organization that Sykes highlights. The
stark contrast between Sykes and DiIulio can be seen in
their analyses of prison riots. Whereas riots for Sykes re-
sulted from tightening control and displacing the real men

---

[13] James B. Jacobs, *Stateville: The Penitentiary in Mass Society,* Chicago:
University of Chicago Press, 1977.
[14] *Governing Prisons*, p. 6.

from the inmate leadership, prison riots for DiIulio were due to insufficient official discipline.

Evidence for these competing theories is mixed. For example, Mark Colvin provides a detailed analysis of the 1980 riot at the Penitentiary of New Mexico. The riot—which caused millions of dollars in property damage and left thirty-three dead—was preceded by the growing role in prison life of younger, more violent inmates. Conflict between inmates and guards was precipitated by a shift in prison management from a "remunerative compliance structure" to a "coercive compliance structure."[15] These trends paralleled the emergence of disorder in New Jersey in the early 1950s. Against this analysis, Bert Useem and his colleagues studied over a dozen prison riots in the 1970s and 1980s. These comparative case studies showed that a breakdown in the administrative order—signaled by escalating violence and escapes—anticipated collective violence in prisons.[16] Sykes's analysis is often contrasted with theories of administrative breakdown, but there is certainly common ground. For both approaches, the legitimacy of officials among inmates—what Sykes would probably distinguish as the "validity" of the custodial regime—is the main ingredient for order. Coercion alone is not enough.

Captives in the Era of the Prison Boom

The two debates surrounding *Captives*—over societal influences on the prison and the orderly effects of penal discipline—acquire special significance in the time of the prison boom. By 2004, the American penal population included more than 2.1 million inmates, a sevenfold increase from 1970. The U.S. incarceration rate had become the highest in the world, exceeding in recent years the rates of its close ri-

[15] Mark Colvin, *The Penitentiary in Crisis: From Accommodation to Riot in New Mexico*, Albany: State University of New York Press, 1992.

[16] Bert Useem and Peter Kimball, *States of Siege: U.S. Prison Riots, 1971–1986*, New York: Oxford University Press, 1989, and Bert Useem, Camille Graham Camp, and George M. Camp, *Resolution of Prison Riots: Strategies and Policies*, New York: Oxford University Press, 1996.

vals, Russia and South Africa. The astonishing growth of the U.S. penal system through the 1980s and the 1990s transformed the contours of American criminal justice. The prison of the early 2000s had become a warehouse for poor young men, embedding the prison deeply in the social inequalities of free society. The prison boom was infused with a politics of discipline that sought order through legitimate violence, not in the informal bases of social cohesion that Sykes emphasized.

The punitive politics driving the prison boom produced a change in the scale of imprisonment and a change in philosophy too. The necessity of custody overwhelmed ambitions for rehabilitation. To be sure, the corrective function of incarceration was always precarious. In the 1950s, decades before the punitive turn in criminal justice policy, Sykes found little practical commitment to rehabilitation. Voicing skepticism that would later broaden into a policy consensus by the 1970s, Sykes observed that

the advocates of confinement as a method of achieving rehabilitation of the criminal have often found themselves in the position of calling for an operation where the target of the scalpel remains unknown.[17]

Prison officials too, Sykes reported, were fighting more of a holding action that attempted to minimize harm rather than ensure reform.[18]
Though the rehabilitative ideal was often diluted in practice, its institutional reality was inscribed in the procedures and agencies for criminal processing. Specific theories of rehabilitation differed, but the guiding principle was one of individualized treatment that gave wide discretion to criminal justice officials. The agencies of probation and parole, the discretionary system of indeterminate sentencing, the juvenile justice system erected on a jurisprudence of dimin-

[17] *SOC*, p. 11.
[18] Ibid., p. 35.

ished capacity were all inspired by the goal of rehabilitation.[19] Inside the prison, a multitude of behavioral, educational, and vocational programs were introduced to set offenders on the path to criminal desistance. David Garland described the rehabilitative project of modern corrections as "penal welfarism," placing the prison alongside public schools, social insurance, and antipoverty policy as one of a number of society's efforts to restore social membership to its fallen citizens.[20]

The punitive turn repudiated penal welfarism, however, and produced more stringent conditions of imprisonment. In 1974, Robert Martinson reported on a comprehensive review of prison rehabilitation programs. In considering the question "what works?" he found the answer was "nothing much," a view later endorsed by the National Research Council.[21] Through the 1980s and 1990s, skepticism about rehabilitation blossomed and school and treatment programs were curtailed. Prison gyms and classrooms made room for new housing units. So-called shock incarceration programs, like boot camps, took in first-time and juvenile offenders. These and many other developments in the conditions of penal confinement have extended the control of the guards and reduced interaction among inmates.

For Malcolm Feeley and Jonathan Simon, these innovations in criminal supervision aimed to corral and control problem populations rather than reform individual offenders. Prison wardens under this new penology were charged more with warehousing inmates than rehabilitation.[22] Mark

[19] David Rothman, *Conscience and Convenience*, rev. ed., New York: Aldine DeGruyter, 2002.

[20] David Garland, *Punishment and Modern Society*, Chicago: University of Chicago Press, 1990.

[21] Robert Martinson, "What Works? Questions and Answers about Prison Reform," *The Public Interest*, Spring 1974, pp. 22–54; Lee Sechrest, Susan O. White, and Elizabeth D. Brown, eds. , *The Rehabilitation of Criminal Offenders: Problems and Prospects,* Washington, D.C.: National Academy of Sciences, 1979.

[22] Malcolm Feeley and Jonathan Simon, "The New Penology: Notes on the Emerging Strategy of Corrections and Its Implications," *Criminology,*

Fleisher's ethnography of Lompoc federal prison describes life under the new penology, in which the driving mission is to incapacitate dangerous and incorrigible offenders. Though the threat of official reprisal is often close at hand, Fleisher emphasizes how seasoned officers resolve conflict by negotiation rather than by "hid[ing] behind the formal discipline system."[23] Guards are told to "follow policy," but this is an admonition to avoid arbitrary violence, rather than to slavishly follow prison rules. Federal prison of the mid-1980s was more tightly organized than state prison of the 1950s, but Sykes's informal sources of social order clearly endure, even under the new penology.[24]

The custodial imperative of the new penology reached its apex with the emergence of supermax prisons in the 1980s. In the 1950s, solitary confinement was reserved as a disciplinary measure, an additional layer of punishment in New Jersey's toughest prison. Today, this most punitive form of incarceration has taken over entire institutions. Termed "supermax," these highest-security prisons are institutions of solitary confinement in which inmates spend twenty-three hours of every day isolated in their cells. Extinguishing all the social interaction at the core of *Captives*, the supermax unit nevertheless houses a social system that tells us much about the dynamics of mass imprisonment. Lorna Rhodes's ethnography of supermax confinement in Washington State, for example, studies not the patterns of interaction among inmates (there are virtually none), but the technologies of confinement, the work of custody staff in maintaining extreme forms of isolation, and the interpreta-

---

Vol. 30, 1992, pp. 449–474. DiIulio's *Governing Prisons* is seen by Feeley and Simon as a managerial manifesto for the new penology.

[23] Mark Fleisher, *Warehousing Violence*, Newbury Park: Sage, 1989.

[24] Other recent field studies of state and federal prisons also describe the negotiated and informal bases of social order: Ann Chih Lin, *Reform in the Making*, Princeton: Princeton University Press, 2000, chapter 2; Dana M. Britton, *At Work in the Iron Cage*, New York: New York University Press, 2003.

tive work of prisoners in a deeply asocial setting.[25] Even here, where total power might appear less defective than in the prison of the 1950s, Rhodes joins Sykes by observing that coercion alone cannot be the primary method of sustaining order. She writes that

custody is where the constraints of prison meet the inmate's will, but sheer force is not the primary method. Administrators sometimes say that the inmates are really in control of the institution. "We just steer them," said one.[26]

Without the inmate's (often minimal) cooperation—which is purchased with some negotiation even in supermax confinement—the prison becomes more violent and dangerous.

In Sykes's time, the prison was an exotic institution that brought into focus rarefied aspects of social life. The self-contained prison society that Sykes described was justified by the low incarceration rates in the fifty years before mass imprisonment. By the 2000s, when imprisonment had become a normal part of the young adulthood of African American men with little schooling, researchers began examining the so-called collateral consequences—the social impact—of the prison in poor urban communities.

Though researchers had previously followed inmates outside the prison gates in search of rehabilitation or recidivism, the new research focuses on incarceration's effects on economic opportunity and families. For example, Donald Braman's ethnography of the poor African American neighborhoods of Washington, D.C., examines how the stigma of incarceration affects prison inmates and their relatives. Braman reports that incarceration largely shields inmates from stigma, while families left in free society must manage

---

[25] Lorna A. Rhodes, *Total Confinement: Madness and Reason in the Maximum Security Prison*, Berkeley: University of California Press, 2004.
[26] Ibid., p. 76.

the shame of imprisonment.[27] Anne Nurse's field research focused on young Californian inmates in their role as fathers separated from wives, girlfriends, and children. In many cases these young men were weakly tied to their children, poorly prepared for fatherhood, and confronted by a hostile web of gender relations.[28] Labor market researchers have begun to study the effects of incarceration on the economic well-being of ex-prisoners. Men released from prison have little access to primary sector jobs and are instead relegated to the secondary labor market of irregular work, low pay, and stagnant wage growth. Devah Pager's field experiments showed that employers overwhelmingly prefer job applicants with clean records over ex-felons, even in the best-case scenario in which ex-felons are clean-cut, well-spoken, educated, and possessing a decent work history.[29]

For this research on the social consequences of incarceration, the prison society extends beyond the correctional facility and into poor neighborhoods. In the era of mass incarceration the prison is not detached from society. It is instead part of the institutional landscape traversed by the urban poor as they move through the life course, to look for work, and form families. Going beyond the earlier prison sociology that saw the stamp of society on the prison, research on collateral consequences shows how the prison is stamped on society, on the lived experience of urban poverty. From this perspective, the prison in the era of mass incarceration has become part of a uniquely American system of social inequality.

In this context, *The Society of Captives* acquires a new significance, not only as a study of prison life, but as an ac-

---

[27] Donald Braman, *Doing Time on the Outside: Incarceration and Family Life in Urban America*, Ann Arbor: University of Michigan Press, 2002. See also the field study by Megan Comfort, "In the Tube at San Quentin: The Secondary Prisonization of Women Visiting Inmates," *Journal of Contemporary Ethnography*, Vol. 32, 2003, pp. 77–107.

[28] Anne Nurse, *Fatherhood Arrested: Parenting from Within the Juvenile Justice System*, Nashville: Vanderbilt University Press, 2002.

[29] Devah Pager, "The Mark of a Criminal Record," *American Journal of Sociology*, Vol. 108, 2003, pp. 937–975.

count of society in which repression is the official strategy for maintaining social order. In Sykes's New Jersey State Prison, repression was organized by prison authorities. In poor inner-city communities in the era of the prison boom, a massive experiment is being deployed in the use of punitive social policy. The prison is just part of a broader effort that also involves enlarged urban police forces, probation and parole agencies, foster care, juvenile justice systems, welfare agencies, and immigration courts. Like the penal system, these other public agencies for the poor rely more on proscription and penalties, and have contributed to the expansion of the penal system. Here we might borrow Loïc Wacquant's "prisonization of the ghetto" to describe the saturation of ghetto life with the formal social control agencies of the state.[30]

In the case of the prisonized ghetto, Sykes reminds us of the defects of total power. For Sykes, a sustainable social order cannot be coerced from above, and must instead promote the local sources of social cohesion. This was the role played by the real men in New Jersey State Prison of the 1950s. If the theory can be generalized, it suggests that intensive policing, incarceration, and the myriad other forms of social control will have only limited effect in the modern ghetto. Indeed, urban sociologists share with Sykes an emphasis on the local social capital that shapes safety and stability in urban neighborhoods. For Mitchell Duneier, these are the sidewalk vendors that form part of the street life of lower Manhattan. For Sudhir Venkatesh, the corporatized street gangs of Robert Taylor Homes in Chicago provide economic support and public safety for local residents. Resembling the real men of New Jersey State Prison, Elijah Anderson's old heads modeled decent and nonviolent behavior in Philadelphia's ghetto neighborhoods. For the urban criminology of Robert Sampson, social order springs from the

---

[30] Loïc Wacquant, "The New 'Peculiar Institution': On the Prison as Surrogate Ghetto," *Theoretical Criminology,* Vol. 4, 2000, pp. 377–389.

collective efficacy of neighbors willing to help out in emergencies.[31] In each of these cases, the social order of cities is found in informal social organization.

Sykes enlivens this work by showing how the informal and indigenous sources of social order are threatened by the expansion of official control. If today's inner city can be likened to Sykes's society of captives, the repressive path to social order risks displacing the local web of social relations that might otherwise promote cohesion. Indeed, the contemporary ghetto—short of jobs and soaked with official supervision—is a negative space like the prison. This is a community of chronic shortage that presents more sanctions than rewards. In this context, Sykes argues, the social order that does emerge is profoundly unstable. Finding its place in the cracks and corners of the negative space—perhaps in the fragile networks of street vendors or gang members—social order remains vulnerable to official efforts at social control. Enduring social stability, it seems, must await the development of a positive space, a real economy of incentives and rewards.

*   *   *   *

Writing in the 1950s, Sykes was unsentimental about prisoners' potential for violence, but more worried about the state's vastly greater capacity for repression. Having returned from war in Europe, writing in the shadow of Nuremberg, and under the canopy of the Cold War, Sykes knew that the specter of totalitarianism was not far away. The pains of imprisonment, he observed, annihilate the person by dissolving individuality and autonomy. In its repressive phase the prison demands accountability. Extraordi-

---

[31] Mitchell Duneier, *Sidewalk*, New York: Farrar, Straus and Giroux, 1999; Sudhir Venkatesh, *American Project: The Rise and Fall of a Modern Ghetto*, Chicago: University of Chicago Press, 2000; Elijah Anderson, *Streetwise: Race, Class, and Change in an Urban Community*, Chicago: University of Chicago Press, 1990; and Robert J. Sampson, Stephen Raudenbush, and Felton Earls, "Neighborhoods and Violent Crime: A Multilevel Study of Collective Efficacy," *Science*, No. 277, 1997, pp. 918–924.

nary acts of will and self-restraint are needed to avoid further punishment under these conditions of exact control and scrutiny. Here, Sykes puts the basic paradox of imprisonment better than most: you cannot promote free will—acting with self-control and foresight—by extinguishing it. In the era of mass incarceration, whole communities are engulfed by this paradox. When the pains of imprisonment are felt not just inside the prison but also in its penumbra, the society of captives is perhaps broader than we ever imagined.

PREFACE

THE "prison problem" would seem to be a hardy perennial, unfortunately, for it has managed to survive every new storm of public indignation and concern. Jeremy Bentham, John Howard, Sir James Mackintosh, Elizabeth Fry—these were but the first of a long series of persons who have raised their voices in protest against the penitentiary, and today the criticisms continue with undiminished force. Yet the problem remains.

It is not my purpose in this book to add to these criticisms, although I too believe that attempting to reform criminals by placing them in prison is based on a fallacy. As George Bernard Shaw has said, common sense alone should prevent our thinking that two blacks make a white. My purpose here, however, has been to examine the prison from a sociological perspective, to see it as an operating social system which can clarify our ideas about man and his behavior, without introducing value judgments either for or against imprisonment. Such analysis must, I believe, precede any program of reform. There are, of course, many dangers in the effort to achieve objectivity on the part of the student of social behavior, and there are a number of writers today who would claim that such effort is not only inherently futile but foolish as well. I disagree with them, however, and in this book I have tried to keep the description and theoretical interpretation of facts apart from my own biases.

Of the many people who have contributed their thought and energy to this book, I would particularly like to thank the members of the Social Science Research Council Committee for the Study of Penal Institutions. My fellow members of this group, consisting of Professors Richard A. Cloward, Donald R. Cressey, George H. Grosser, Frank E. Hartung, Richard

McCleery, and Lloyd E. Ohlin, are well aware of my indebtedness. I would also like to express my appreciation to my colleagues at Princeton University: Professors Melvin M. Tumin, Wilbert E. Moore, Sheldon E. Messinger, and Frederick F. Stephan. In addition, Professor Arnold Feldman of the University of Delaware and Hugh Watts have been of inestimable help. Finally, I should like to express my gratitude to Dr. F. L. Bixby and Dr. Lloyd W. McCorkle of the New Jersey State Department of Institutions and Agencies who provided an unfailing source of encouragement.

GRESHAM M. SYKES
Princeton University

May 1, 1958

INTRODUCTION

ALTHOUGH THE PRACTICE of placing men in custody is probably as old as society itself, only within the last three hundred years or so has custody emerged as a major weapon of the State for dealing with the criminal. In earlier eras imprisonment was mainly a period in limbo, a way-station in the legal process where the suspected offender looked forward to the hangman's noose or the lash. As late as 1771 the French jurist Jousse could claim that imprisonment was simply a means of holding the suspected criminal before trial and not a method of punishment;[1] and not until the beginning of the 19th Century did imprisonment achieve its present eminence as a major penal sanction.

A number of forces have been suggested as the well-springs of this shift in perspective. The growth of humanitarian ideals, it is argued, made imprisonment far more appealing than the hangings, floggings, burnings, and mutilations which society had used as its answers to crime in the past. The spread of personal liberty made it possible to view the loss of liberty as a serious deterrent. The philosophy of the Enlightenment aided the belief that at long last society could make the punishment fit the crime by rationally assigning sentences of various lengths with the handy metric of time. And, according to one school of thought, a society caught up in an industrial revolution must have found the combination of punishment and profitable penal labor irresistibly attractive.[2]

[1] Thorsten Sellin, "Imprisonment," in *Encyclopaedia of the Social Sciences*, Edwin R. A. Seligman (ed.), New York: Macmillan Company, 1932.

[2] For an excellent, brief account of changes in penal policy, see Edwin H. Sutherland, *Principles of Criminology* (revised by Donald R. Cressey), New York: J. B. Lippincott Company 1955, Chapter Fourteen.

Whatever the cause—*Zeitgeist*, expediency or plain charity —the shift occurred. The prisons of the 18th and 19th Centuries replaced the dungeons and detention rooms of prior years. The criminal was no longer simply to be killed, tortured and dismissed, or thrust beyond the pale in the exile of transportation. Now he was also to be encapsulated in the body of the State.

The fact that today we confine large masses of criminals for long periods is so obvious that we are apt to overlook its significance: Society has created communities containing hundreds or thousands of individuals working, eating, sleeping, and living together for years on end. Custody is no longer represented by a galley slave chained to his oar, a handful of suspects briefly held, an individual suddenly run wild and temporarily restrained, or the lone political prisoner. Rather, custody is many individuals bound together for long intervals. Such aggregates enduring through time must inevitably give rise to a social system—not simply the social order decreed by the custodians, but also the social order which grows up more informally as men interact in meeting the problems posed by their particular environment. In attempting, then, to understand the meaning of imprisonment, we must see prison life as something more than a matter of walls and bars, of cells and locks. We must see the prison as a society within a society.[3]

II

The institutions in which criminals are confined in the United States today show a great variety, both in terms of their publicly announced procedures and their actual performance. There are prisons for men and for women, for federal offenders and for state offenders, for adults and for juveniles. Institutions differ with respect to the extent of the psychiatric

[3] A rigorous definition of the word society might not include the social system of the prison. (See Marion J. Levy, Jr., *The Structure of Society*, Princeton, New Jersey: Princeton University Press, 1952, pp. 112-113.) Nonetheless, the prison has many of the characteristics commonly attributed to a society and it is fruitful to examine it from this point of view.

services which they provide, the nature of their work program, the stringency of custody, the number of inmates, and so on. And on top of this variation, based on a deliberately designed penal policy, we find still other differences stemming from the exigencies of daily events and the personal philosophies of those charged with the responsibility of administering places of confinement.

Yet in spite of this diversity it is not inconsistent to say that the observer must be struck by the basic similarities which exist among custodial institutions, for there seems to be a remarkable tendency to override the variations of time, place, and purpose. Prisons are apt to present a common social structure. Perhaps this is due to a diffusion of ideas, customs, and laws; perhaps it is a matter of similar social structures arising independently from attempts to solve much the same problems. Most probably it is some combination of both. In any case, prisons appear to form a group of social systems differing in detail but alike in their fundamental processes, a genus or family of sociological phenomena.

This book is concerned with a so-called maximum security prison, that is, a custodial institution reserved for adult male criminals who are thought to require extremely close supervision and control. Much attention has been devoted to maximum security prisons in terms of their influence on the criminality of the confined offender *after* he has been released, for in this progressive age, it is said, we place the criminal in prison not in the spirit of revenge, but in the fond hope that the experience will lead him to refrain from criminal behavior in the future. This interest in the aftermath of imprisonment has been based in part on humanitarian motives and, in part, on the pressing needs of an immediate social problem. The resulting literature on recidivism and performance on parole has been of great value, but unfortunately the objective description and analysis of the prison experience itself has remained somewhat neglected.[4] All too often the

---

[4] The pioneering work of Donald Clemmer (*The Prison Community*, Boston: The Christopher Publishing House, 1940) stands out as one of

reports on life in prison consist of sensational exposes, anecdotes, or anguished cries of protest, the product of men intent on advancing a cause or catering to the curious. Yet for the social scientists the effect of imprisonment on the behavior of the criminal after he is released is only one facet of the prison's claim to attention, and the custodial institution—as a special type of social system—is a significant object of study in its own right.

The student of human behavior can find many theoretical issues suddenly illuminated by examining this small-scale society where numerous features of the free community have been drastically changed. In the prison, for example, we find the activity of work—so central to the scheme of things in modern industrial society—transfigured by the realities of prison servitude. Race relations take on new forms in the custodial institution where the ratio between Negroes and whites frequently approaches unity and both groups live under conditions of enforced equality. In the prison, as in war, we find men without women and norms concerning the masculine role and the endurance of sexual frustrations take on new guises. In the prison the obvious symbols of social status have been largely stripped away and we find new hierarchies with new symbols coming into play. But what is most important, perhaps, is the fact that the *maximum security prison represents a social system in which an attempt is made to create and maintain total or almost total social control.*

The detailed regulations extending into every area of the individual's life, the constant surveillance, the concentration of power into the hands of a ruling few, the wide gulf between the rulers and the ruled—all are elements of what we would usually call a totalitarian regime.[5] The threat of force lies close beneath the surface of the custodial institution and it is the invisible fist rather than Adam Smith's invisible hand

---

the few full-length portraits of an American prison seen from a sociological perspective.

[5] Cf. N. A. Polanski, "The Prison as an Autocracy," *Journal of Criminal Law and Criminology*, 33, pp. 16-22, May-June 1942.

which regulates much of the prisoner's activity. The prison official is a bureaucrat, but he is a bureaucrat with a gun.

The combination is a fearful one, for it is the basis of the calculated atrocities of the concentration camp and the ruthless exploitation of the Soviet *lager*. It is true that the American maximum security prison is different from these in terms of the nature of the tasks which the prison seeks to perform, the characteristics of the officials who direct those tasks, and the matrix of the democratic community in which the prison is embedded. The prison is not planned with an eye to annihilating its captive population—either physically or psychologically—nor is it designed to wring the last ounce of effort from an expendable labor force. Instead, it pursues an odd combination of confinement, internal order, self-maintenance, punishment, and reformation, all within a framework of means sharply limited by law, public opinion, and the attitudes of the custodians themselves. None the less, attempts to exercise total social control through the use of a bureaucratically organized administrative staff would all seem to be cut on much the same pattern and the prison appears to offer many clues to the structure and functioning of the new leviathan.

In an era when a system of total power has changed from a nightmare of what the future might be like to a reality experienced by millions, questions concerning the theory and practice of total power take on a new urgency. Do systems of total power contain inherent pathologies, in the sense that there are strains and tensions in the structure which must inevitably crack the monolithic concentration of power?[6] Do types of resistance such as apathy, corruption, and the hard bedrock of informal human ties which are present in every social system curtail the power of the rulers?[7] Or is total power a juggernaut capable of crushing all opposition, a form of

[6] Cf. Karl Deutsch, "Cracks in the Monolith," in *Totalitarianism*, Carl J. Friedrich (ed.), Cambridge, Mass.: Harvard University Press, 1954, pp. 308-333.

[7] Cf. David Riesman, "Some Observations on the Limits of Totalitarian Power," in *Individualism Reconsidered*, Glencoe, Ill.: The Free Press, 1954.

social organization as viable as more democratic modes? What values are created among the rulers and the ruled? How does living in a system of complete social control affect the personality of the rulers and the ruled?

Perhaps these and similar issues cannot be solved at the most general level, in the sense that we can develop statements which are valid for any system of total power. Perhaps the problem of total power is so huge in its implications and so varied in its manifestations that it defies universal answers. This, however, is a question to be settled by experience and not by fiat. In the meantime, we can examine particular types of total power and hope to enlarge our understanding of the general problem through the knowledge gained from the specific case. Perhaps in this way the maximum security prison can supply a prism through which we can see the spectrum of forces at work when social control nears its extreme.

III

This study, then, concerns itself with a single system of total power—the social system of the New Jersey State Maximum Security Prison. Here more than 300 custodial, clerical, and professional state employees are organized into bureaucratic administrative staff charged with the duty of governing approximately 1,200 adult male criminals held in confinement for periods of time ranging from one year to life.

The State of New Jersey has in actuality three major penal institutions for adult male criminals. First, there is a prison farm at Rahway, an institution to which "the more stable and tractable prisoners may be transferred after study and classification at the main Prison."[8] Second, there is a prison farm at Leesburg, "a minimum security unit to which the most trustworthy of the Prison population are transferred to furnish labor for extensive farming and canning operations."[9] It is, however, the maximum security prison, located

---

[8] New Jersey, Department of Institutions and Agencies Research Bulletin No. 18, "Two Thousand State Prisoners in New Jersey," Trenton, New Jersey, May 1954.

[9] *Ibid.*

in the city of Trenton, which is the focus of our attention and which has been described in official publications as an institution for the detention of "older, more serious, and more recalcitrant male offenders with poor records and long sentences."[10] All three institutions are under the jurisdiction of the Division of Correction, which is in turn subordinate to the Department of Institutions and Agencies. Until the new state constitution was adopted in 1947, the Principal Keeper (Warden of the Trenton Prison) was appointed by the Governor. Since 1951, the authority to appoint the incumbent of the office has resided in the Board of Managers of the Trenton Prison, subject to the approval of the State Board of Control which exercises broad authority over the Department of Institutions and Agencies. The change was designed to "take the Prison out of politics" and to a certain extent it has been successful.

In October 1954, a survey of the inmate population of the New Jersey State Maximum Security Prison indicated that the crimes which brought these men to the institution ranged from murder to desertion, but four general categories accounted for the great majority of offenders: 24 percent had been convicted of felonious homicide, 24 percent of burglary, 20 percent of robbery, and 12 percent of larceny in a variety of forms. The median age of the inmates was 35 years and 63 percent had had less than nine years of formal schooling. Negroes comprised approximately 38 percent of the group. The reports of the institution's psychologist indicated that 55 percent of the prisoners were average or better in mental level, the remainder being classified as dull normal, inferior, borderline, or deficient. In the matter of psychological abnormality, 24 percent were said to have "no psychosis," 25 percent were labelled "psychopathic personality," and 30 percent were diagnosed as "constitutional defective"; the terms epileptic, chronic alchoholic, constitutional inferior, and neurotic exhausted the rest. A large share—65 percent—had experienced confinement in a penal institution for one year or

10 *Ibid.*

more prior to their present imprisonment and only 16 percent exhibited no previous criminal record. Approximately one half of the inmates had been in prison for two years or more as part of their current sentence, and 25 percent could look forward to being detained on their release for questioning by the police and possible trial in connection with other crimes. In these crude terms, at least, the population of the Trenton Prison does not appear to differ markedly from the inmate population of maximum security prisons in other states; and it is this population which the prison officials must lead into the usages of conformity.

Of course, the New Jersey State Prison undoubtedly differs from other maximum security institutions in certain respects, such as the proportion of inmates from urban centers, the age of the buildings, the details of the custodial regime, and so on. Such differences are sure to loom large in the minds of those intimately involved in the administration of particular institutions; and such differences must make us cautious in attempting to generalize. Yet it seems that the similarity of the New Jersey State Prison to the other institutions—in terms of social structure—is far more outstanding than the dissimilarity.[11]

IV

When the plans for this study were first constructed, an effort was made to develop a small number of relatively specific hypotheses dealing with the causes and effects of different types of adjustment to the prison environment. As the problem was examined further, however, it became clear that such an effort was somewhat premature; there was far too little knowledge of the variety of roles played by criminals in prison and even less knowledge of how these roles were related to one another and to the social order which the

[11] This was brought out with particular sharpness in a conference sponsored by the Social Science Research Council in 1955 and 1956, in which a number of sociologists studying a variety of institutions were able to compare their findings in detail.

custodians attempted to create in the pursuit of their assigned tasks. In other words, there was a good deal of ignorance about the prison as a social system—as a complex set of interrelated patterns of social behavior—and without a fuller knowledge of the social structure of the prison as a whole, conclusions concerning the causes and effects of particular reactions could be grossly misleading. It was decided, therefore, that an exploratory study of the prison as a social system would be more valuable than the testing of a limited number of propositions whose context remained in doubt.

It must be admitted, however, that the social system of the prison is a difficult thing to uncover. Criminals in the custodial institution seldom keep written records setting forth the ideology of the inmate population, its myths or its mores. The informant is apt to be defined as a "rat" or a "squealer" and the observer from the free community is viewed with suspicion. Language presents no great barrier, it is true, but there is an argot to be mastered and a misused term marks you off as a pretender. And in this struggle to gain access to the thoughts and life of captives and captors, the social scientist often faces the subtle opposition of the officials, for they too have a stake in the game of acquiring knowledge. Careers, jobs, and reputations depend on the efficient functioning of the prison and what is a familiar administrative problem for the prison bureaucracy can become a scandal of mismanagement if it is made public. The observer of the prison, then, must deal with the difficulties of any observer who wishes to glimpse reality rather than illustrations for a preconception, but he has the additional hazard of working in an area where disclosure may be costly.

Fortunately, the ready cooperation and encouragement of the officials of the New Jersey State Maximum Security Prison did much to eliminate the problem of administrative reticence: Official files, standard operating procedures, and other records were made freely available. In addition, the open-handed support of the prison administration made it possible to interview guards, civilian work supervisors, and inmates under conditions making for a good deal of frankness. The anonymity of those who provided information could be assured and men could be questioned on the job, in their cells, in the recreation hall, and so on. There remained, of course, many barriers to easy communication between the writer and both the custodians of the institution and their captives, for a prison is founded in part on secrecy and the observer from the free community is inevitably defined as an intruder, at least initially. Gradually, however, over a period of three years, it was possible to become redefined as a more or less neutral figure in the schismatic struggles which split the prison and much of this reluctance to talk was overcome.[12]

[12] See Appendix A.

THE SOCIETY OF CAPTIVES

CHAPTER ONE

THE PRISON AND ITS SETTING

WHEN THE New Jersey State Maximum Security Prison was first built in the last decade of the 18th Century, it was surrounded by open fields beyond the limits of Trenton. The town, however, developed into a city and today the dwelling houses of the lower or lower-middle class border the prison on three sides and railroad tracks mark the fourth. A massive wall 20 feet high separates the free community from the prisoners, serving not only as the final barrier to escape but also as a symbol of society's rejection—for this is a fort to keep the enemy within rather than without.[1]

From the street outside the prison you can see the guards in their towers on the wall. Each is armed with a shotgun, a revolver, and gas grenades to quell a riot or strike down the inmate desperate enough to attempt escape. But these disturbances occur infrequently; the last riot took place in 1952 and no one has tried to scale the wall for more than a decade. The guard in his tower holds a position organized around the theme of potential crisis, the possible event made improbable by vigilance. It is a theme which we will encounter often in our examination of the prison.

Within the prison wall lie 13 1/2 acres of buildings, yards, and passageways. Cellblocks, offices, barber shops, laundry, industrial shops, chapel, exercise yards, dining halls, kitchens, and the death house are jammed together or piled one on

[1] For a full history of the Trenton Prison, see Harry Elmer Barnes, *A History of the Penal, Reformatory, and Correctional Institutions of the State of New Jersey*, Trenton, New Jersey: MacCrellish & Quigley Company, 1918.

top of the other, for this community of more than 1,500 individuals must be squeezed into an area not much larger than several city blocks. The society of prisoners, however, is not only physically compressed; it is psychologically compressed as well, since prisoners live in an enforced intimacy where each man's behavior is subject both to the constant scrutiny of his fellow captives and the surveillance of the custodians. It is not solitude that plagues the prisoner but life *en masse*.

The main entrance to the prison is a small steel door with a slot of bullet-proof glass, set in the eastern wall. After passing through this portal the newly arrived inmate is led down a hall lined on both sides with administrative offices—an area labelled the Front House in the argot of the captives. Ahead of him lies another steel door and still another; and only after the last of these has shut behind him does he stand within the prison proper. Before he leaves the outer hall he is taken to a room where he is stripped and searched. His age, name, crime, sentence, and other information are duly recorded; his civilian possessions are taken away and he puts on the prison uniform. Thus he enters the custodial institution, a poor man in terms of material goods; later he will be given other things (a change of clothing, a cup, a spoon, blankets, etc.), but they will place him only just above the line of bare necessity. The prisoner is supposed to live in poverty as a matter of public policy, an unwilling monk of the 20th Century.

On the other side of the third steel door lies the Center— a large chamber which serves as the hub of the official communication system. This is the check point which all men must pass in moving about the institution; it is the place where extra weapons are stored, the constant counts of the inmate population are received, and the shifts of guards coming on duty at eight-hour intervals assemble for roll call and assignment of duties. It is said that whoever controls the Center controls the prison, for the reins of government are gathered here; and like many seats of government it has

4

come to take on a symbolic quality transcending its physical details. In the vocabulary of the inmates, a *center man* is a prisoner who allies himself too blatantly with the world of the custodians; and in the eyes of the officials, arrogance or disrespect in the Center has a special significance as an affront to legitimate authority.

Radiating from the Center, in a ground plan reminiscent of Vilain's *Maison de Force*,[2] are the cellblocks or wings which house the society of captives. A typical cellblock contains two banks of cells set back to back, rising from floor to ceiling in the center of the building, and it is in one of these honey-combed structures that the inmate lives for the duration of his sentence. Since the prison has grown piecemeal over a period of more than one hundred years, the cellblocks differ in the details of their construction, such as the size and number of the cells they contain, the nature of the locking devices for the cell doors or grills, and the means of ventilation. The largest cells in the institution are 15 feet long, 7 1/2 feet wide, and about 10 feet high; the smallest are 7 1/2 feet long, 4 1/2 feet wide, and 7 feet high. Regardless of their size, the official furnishings of these compartments are harshly Spartan: a toilet, a washbowl, a bed, a table, a footlocker, shelves, a set of earphones for the prison radio, and a single electric light hanging from the ceiling comprise the list.

Hot in the summer and cold in the winter, cramped and barren, the stone and steel cellblock would seem to express the full nature of imprisonment as seen in the popular fancy. Indeed, if men in prison were locked forever in their cells, shut off from all intercourse with each other, and deprived of all activities of normal life, the dimensions of the cell would be the alpha and omega of life in prison. Like so many animals in their cages, the inmate population would be an aggregate rather than a social group, a mass of isolates rather than a society. The duties of the officials would consist prima-

2 Harry Elmer Barnes and Negley K. Teeters, *New Horizons in Criminology*, New York: Prentice-Hall, Inc., 1952, pp. 384-385.

rily of administering to the physiological needs of their captives in their individual enclosures and the prisoner would interact only with himself.

In fact, however, prisoners are released from their cells each day to engage in a variety of activities under the direction and supervision of the custodians. Inmates are freed from their cells and marched to the messhall for breakfast, lunch, and dinner. Inmates are freed from their cells to perform the innumerable chores involved in the daily round of institutional existence. Stoking fires, cooking, barbering, washing clothes, sweeping, working as hospital orderlies—all are necessary duties which are carried out by prisoners. Inmates are freed from their cells to exercise in the Yard, to work in the industrial shops, to watch television in the recreation hall, to study in the prison school, to attend religious services. It is these patterns of release and reconfinement which set the stage for a wide range of social interaction between inmate and inmate and guard and inmate; and in this interaction we can begin to see the realities of the prison social system emerge.

In a very fundamental sense, a man perpetually locked by himself in a cage is no longer a man at all; rather, he is a semi-human object, an organism with a number. The identity of the individual, both to himself and to others, is largely compounded of the web of symbolic communications by which he is linked to the external world; and as Kingsley Davis has pointed out, ". . . the structure of the human personality is so much a product of social interaction that when this interaction ceases it tends to decay."[3] It was the recognition of this fact that played a large part in the abandonment of solitary confinement for the general inmate population of the American prison. Humanitarian motives, combined with a growing doubt about the efficacy of solitude and meditation as means of reform, led to a search for alternatives to isolation, in New Jersey as elsewhere. Emil Frankel, in reviewing the development of penal philosophy in New Jersey over a 250-year period, notes that:

[3] Kingsley Davis, *Human Society*, New York: The Macmillan Company, 1949, p. 152.

In his annual report of 1838, the Keeper admitted that . . . solitary confinement apparently had little influence in decreasing the amount of crime committed within the state. And his annual report for 1839 contained an admirable analysis of the fundamental defects in the system of solitary confinement on the physical health of the prisoners through the impossibility of taking normal methods of exercise. But even worse was its effects upon the mental health of the prisoners, it leading to solitary vices and mental degeneration. The choice between the congregate and solitary type of confinement, he held, was fundamentally the problem as to whether vicious association is more to be deplored than mental and physical deterioration.[4]

In addition, there was the constant social demand to reduce the financial burden of imprisonment on the free community to a minimum—a demand ill met by keeping the inmate locked in his cell both day and night. Today, then, solitary confinement is used in the New Jersey State Maximum Security Prison only for those prisoners who are being punished for infractions of the prison rules and it represents the ultimate penalty that the custodians can inflict rather than the common fate of the man in custody. Yet if the prison officials no longer force their captives to remain constantly within the confines of their cells, neither do they permit them to roam freely within the limits set by the wall and its armed guards. In the eyes of the custodians, such a course is prohibited by the elementary requirements of security and the need to maintain order; the prison exists in an uneasy compromise of liberty and restraint.

II

When we examine the physical structure of the prison the most striking feature is, perhaps, its drabness. It has that "institutional" look shared by police stations, hospitals, orphan asylums, and similar public buildings—a Kafka-like atmosphere compounded of naked electric lights, echoing corridors, walls encrusted with the paint of decades, and the stale air of rooms shut up too long.

[4] Emil Frankel, "Crime Treatment in New Jersey, 1668-1934," *Journal of Criminal Law and Criminology*, Vol. xxviii, No. 1, May-June 1937, pp. 98-99.

7

Yet the New Jersey State Prison does not represent acute physical discomfort, nor is there evidence of shockingly bad living conditions. Rather, it gives the impression of a grinding dullness, an existence lacking the amenities of life we take for granted, but an existence which is still tolerable. In this sense, the physical conditions of life in prison would seem to reflect a sort of half-hearted or indecisive punishment, the imposition of deprivation by indifference or forgetfulness rather than by intent. And in fact large segments of our society would much prefer to forget the confined offender, for no matter how just imprisonment may be, the free community is reluctant to face the conclusion that some men must be held in bondage for the larger good. The prison wall, then, does more than help prevent escape; it also hides the prisoners from society. If the inmate population is shut in, the free community is shut out, and the vision of men held in custody is, in part, prevented from arising to prick the conscience of those who abide by the social rules.

In reality, of course, the prison wall is far more permeable than it appears, not in terms of escape—which we will consider later—but in terms of the relationships between the prison social system and the larger society in which it rests. The prison is not an autonomous system of power; rather, it is an instrument of the State, shaped by its social environment, and we must keep this simple truth in mind if we are to understand the prison. It reacts to and is acted upon by the free community as various groups struggle to advance their interests. At certain times, as in the case of riots, the inmates can capture the attention of the public; and indeed disturbances within the walls must often be viewed as highly dramatic efforts to communicate with the outside world, efforts in which confined criminals pass over the heads of their captors to appeal to a new audience. At other times the flow of communications is reversed and the prison authorities find themselves receiving demands raised by a variety of business, political, religious, ethnic, and welfare interest groups. In addition, there is the fact that the personnel of the prison—both the inmates and

8

custodians—are drawn from the free community, whether voluntarily or involuntarily, and they bring with them the attitudes, beliefs, and values of this larger world. The prison, as a social system, does not exist in isolation any more than the criminal within the prison exists in isolation as an individual; and the institution and its setting are inextricably mixed despite the definite boundary of the wall.

III

Lying somewhere between total annihilation of the offender on one hand and warning or forgiveness on the other, imprisonment is generally viewed as the appropriate consequence of most serious crimes. The issue is put more bluntly by prisoners themselves in their aphorism, "If you can't pull the time, don't pull the crime," but the thought is much the same.

Yet why is imprisonment appropriate? On what grounds is imprisonment justified? It is a cliché of modern penology that placing the offender in prison is for the purposes of punishment, deterrence, and reform. There is a beguiling neatness and simplicity about this three-pronged aim but it requires examination. The social system of the New Jersey State Maximum Security Prison lies in a philosophical environment as well as a physical one and the nature of the prison's social system only becomes clear when we understand the rationale on which it is based.

The idea of punishment as the purpose of imprisonment is plain enough—the person who has committed a wrong or hurt must suffer in return. The State, through its agent the prison, is entitled if not morally obligated to hurt the individual who has broken the criminal law, since a crime is by definition a wrong committed against the State. Imprisonment should be punishment, not only by depriving the individual of his liberty, but also by imposing painful conditions under which the prisoner must live within the walls.

Now it is true that there are few persons directly concerned with handling the offender who will advance this

9

view of the prison's purpose as baldly as we have stated it here. Penologists, prison psychiatrists, prison administrators, judges —all are far more apt to claim that we do not place the criminal in prison to secure retribution but to accomplish better things. Yet there is some reason to doubt that this denial of punishment as a legitimate aim of imprisonment accurately reflects the opinions of the general public. However harsh an insistence on retribution may appear to be, it cannot be ignored as a social force shaping the nature of the penal institution, whether in the form of community reactions to accusations of "coddling" prisoners or the construction of budgets by the state legislators.

The idea of deterrence as the aim of imprisonment is somewhat more complicated, for the argument contains three parts which need to be treated separately. First, it is claimed that for those who have been imprisoned the experience is (or should be) sufficiently distasteful to convince them that crime had best be avoided in the future. This decision to forego crime is not expected to come from a change in the attitudes and values concerning the wrongness of crime. Rather, it supposedly flows from a sharpened awareness of the penalties attached to wrongdoing. Second, it is argued that imprisonment is important as a deterrent not for the individual who has committed a crime and who has been placed in prison but for the great mass of citizens who totter on the edge. The image of the prison is supposed to check errant impulses, and again it is fear rather than morality which is expected to guide the individual in his action. Third, there is the assertion that the deterrent effect of imprisonment is largely a matter of keeping known criminals temporarily out of circulation and the major aim of imprisonment is to keep offenders within the walls where they cannot prey on the free community, at least for the moment.

Like those who argue for imprisonment as retribution, the adherents of imprisonment as deterrence tend to support those polices which would make life in prison painful, with the possible exception of those who argue for simple custody

10

alone.[5] They are faced with a moral dilemma when it comes to justifying punishment for the criminal in order to deter the noncriminal, for as Morris Cohen has pointed out, we feel uneasiness in hurting Peter to keep Paul honest. A more serious problem, however, is presented by the fact that the view of imprisonment as deterrence is based on a hypothetical, complicated cause-and-effect relationship. Does the prison experience actually induce the criminal to refrain from wrong-doing through fear of another period in custody? Does the image of the prison, for those who have never been within its walls, really check the potential criminal in mid-act? Affirmative answers to these questions must be secured before the use of imprisonment for the purpose of deterrence is rationally justified and this has proven to be no easy task. The usual procedure has been to make the common-sense assumption that men are rarely so good by either nature or training that they will always conform to the law without the threat of the pains of imprisonment in the background. For those who are too humanitarian to claim vengeance as the goal of confinement and too cynical, perhaps, to hope for real reform in the majority of cases, the objective of deterrence offers a comfortable compromise.

When we turn to the idea of imprisonment as reform, it is clear that there are few who will quarrel with such a desirable goal—the disputes center on how it can be accomplished, if at all. In seeking to use imprisonment for the rehabilitation of the offender, the aim is to eradicate those causes of crime which lie within the individual and imprisonment is commonly regarded as a device to hold the patient still long enough so that this can be achieved.

Unfortunately, the advocates of confinement as a method of achieving rehabilitation of the criminal have often found themselves in the position of calling for an operation where the target of the scalpel remains unknown. In recent years, with the rise of sociological and psychological interpretations

---

[5] It is possible that the criminal could be deterred from crime by being rewarded. This is a possibility that society has hesitated to explore despite the precedent of *Danegelt*.

11

of human behavior, the search for causal factors underlying criminality has grown more sophisticated but the answer remains almost as elusive as before. Yet in spite of the confusion in this area, there are many students of the problem who believe that the reformation of the offender requires a profound change in the individual's personality and that this change can be won only by surrounding the prisoner with a "permissive" or "supportive" social atmosphere.[6] For those devoted to a psychiatric view of criminal behavior, psychotherapy in individual or group sessions is often advanced as the most hopeful procedure; for those with a more sociological bent, self-government, meaningful work, and education are frequently claimed as minimal steps in the direction of reformation. Both factions—divergent though they may be in their theoretical arguments—are apt to agree that the punishing features of imprisonment should be reduced or eliminated if efforts at rehabilitation are to be effective.

It would be interesting to speculate about where these different ideas concerning the proper objectives of imprisonment are lodged in society, the extent to which they form organized ideologies rather than random opinions, and the amount of power behind them. For the moment, however, it is sufficient to point out that the New Jersey State Prison—like all prisons in the United States—is called upon to pursue not one task but several and that these tasks are not easily balanced in a coherent policy. We have called these diverse ideas about the proper aims of imprisonment the philosophical setting of the prison and in the next chapter we shall turn to the translation of these ideas into organizational rules and procedures.

6 The possibility of reforming the criminal with so-called brainwashing techniques, like the possibility of deterrence through rewards, has received little attention.

CHAPTER TWO

THE REGIME OF THE CUSTODIANS

TO SAY THAT MAN is a social animal is also to say that man never lives in a world completely of his own choosing. He is always confronted with the fact that there are others who attempt to make him conform to rules and procedures and he must somehow come to grips with these external demands. He may accept them in whole or in part, turning them into demands which he places on himself, or he may reject them and try to avoid the consequences; yet he can never completely ignore them.

Our concern now is with the social order which the custodians of the New Jersey State Prison attempt to impose on their captives—the massive body of regulations which is erected as a blueprint for behavior within the prison and to which the inmate must respond. This social order (not yet a reality but a statement of what should be) represents a means, a method of achieving certain goals or accomplishing certain tasks; and, as we have pointed out before, the nature of this social order becomes clear only when we understand the ends it is supposed to serve. We will find, however, that the relationships between means and ends in prison are far from simple.

We have indicated that the prison is an instrument of the State, an organization designed to accomplish the desires of society with respect to the convicted criminal. But such a statement is, after all, only an analogy and we must not view the prison as a machine which simply and automatically translates the dictates of society into action. The tasks assigned

13

to the prison must be given priorities; general social objectives must be transformed into specific organizational aims; assumptions must be made about the nature of the criminal and his reactions to confinement; and the limitations placed by society on what the prison can do in pursuit of its mission must be taken into account. In short, the regime which the custodians struggle to impose on the inmate population may indeed be a means of fulfilling the objectives allotted by the larger social order and only becomes explicable in light of these objectives. But the rules and routines of the prison officials represent a choice among alternative means and we must examine the basis of this choice as well as the objectives themselves.

II

It is true that keeping criminals confined can be agreed on as a necessary measure whether retribution, deterrence, or reform is taken as the only proper aim of imprisonment. Being held in custody can, as I have indicated, be viewed as a means of paying back the offender, a method of discouraging the actual or potential criminal, or a device for maintaining access to the patient. Beyond this point, however, the translation of general social tasks into specific organizational procedures runs into difficulties.

First, there is the question of precisely what steps must be taken to insure custody. The difficulties of holding men against their will are commonly recognized, it is true, and as James V. Bennett, Director of the Federal Bureau of Prisons, has pointed out:

When one takes into consideration the antiquity of most prisons, the flimsiness of some prison structures, the Rube Goldberg character of the locking devices, the hit or miss standards used in selecting men for "trusty" assignments, the extent of overcrowding, personnel shortages, and the increasingly more desperate character of the offender, there are few enough escapes.[1]

[1] James V. Bennett, "Evaluating a Prison," *The Annals of the American Academy of Political and Social Science*, Vol. 293, May 1954 p. 11.

But there are many critics who believe that far too great an emphasis is placed on custody and that the many measures used to prevent escapes constitute a backward, irrational ritual. Those who stress custody are, from this point of view, typical examples of the "bureaucratic personality," individuals who have elevated a means to the status of an end,[2] and custodial routines are simply the residue of a punitive orientation toward the criminal, the contaminated man. The endless precautions, the constant counting of the inmate population, the myriad regulations, the institutionalized suspicion of the periodic searches—these, it is held, are the expression of groundless fears and hatreds rather than reason. Criticism is not actually directed against custody per se but against precautions to prevent escapes which are carried too far; and in solving this problem, prison officials responsible for the security of the institution may find themselves cast willy-nilly into the role of offering bullheaded opposition to progress in penal methods.[3]

Second, there is the question of the standard of living which is to be accorded the prisoner. Those who hold that retribution or deterrence should be the primary task of the prison are inclined to believed that the mere loss of liberty is insufficiently painful to accomplish these ends. The inmate must be made to suffer within the walls, not through the use of the thumbscrew, the rack, or the starvation diet which have been barred as forms of cruel and unusual punishment since the 18th Century, but by a series of deprivations which will clearly demonstrate the advantages of remaining within the law or which will underline the condemnation of criminal behavior. Those, however, who hold that reformation is the major aim of imprisonment—who feel that if the custodial institution fails to reform it fails altogether—are apt to argue

[2] Robert K. Merton, "Bureaucratic Structure and Personality," in *Social Theory and Social Structure*, Glencoe, Ill.: The Free Press, 1949.

[3] The argument is often intensified by the fact that in the prison those charged with the duty of custody and those given the duty of reforming the criminal are frequently drawn from widely different social, economic and intellectual backgrounds and possess disparate degrees of experience in custodial institutions.

15

that such additional penalties present an insuperable barrier to therapy. Repression within the prison simply breeds new antagonisms, creating a situation which is almost completely antithetical to modern concepts of psychiatric care. This viewpoint receives additional support from those who would make life in prison less painful or frustrating on humanitarian grounds alone, regardless of whether or not a more "permissive" and "supportive" atmosphere advances or hinders the work of rehabilitation.

Third, men in the maximum security prison must somehow be supported and the traditional solution has been that inmates should support themselves as far as possible. Yet this raises a number of difficult issues, for the solution has been an uneasy one: The State views the labor of prisoners with deep ambivalence. The criminal in the custodial institution is in a position somewhat like that of a wayward son who is forced to work by a stern father. The troublesome youth may not earn his keep, but at least he is to be employed at honest labor; and if his earnings make up only a portion of his expenses, that is better than nothing at all. It should not surprise us if the parent in our simile is motivated by a curious blend of economic self-interest, faith in the efficacy of work as a means of spiritual salvation, and a basic, hostile feeling that no man should escape the burden of supporting himself by the sweat of his brow. Similar forces are perhaps at work when society demands that the custodial institution take on the appearance of a self-sustaining community. The organization of the inmate population into a labor force capable of supporting itself may, however, create serious custodial problems—in addition to eliciting cries of outrage from private enterprise in the free community.[4] Strict concern for custody or a view of work as part of the criminal's punishment can destroy a program of efficient production. And using work as a means of resocializing the adult offender may be

[4] For an illuminating discussion of prison labor, see Edwin H. Sutherland, *Principles of Criminology*, (revised by Donald R. Cressey), New York: J. B. Lippincott Company, 1955, Chapter Twenty-Five.

diametrically opposed to both economic and custodial considerations.

A fourth problem in accommodating the multiple tasks assigned the prison revolves around the issue of internal order. If a prisoner in solitary confinement smashes his head against the wall, it is an individual madness; if he refuses to eat or bathe himself, his rebellion stops short with the limits of his cell. In the maximum security prison, however, the maintenance of order is far more complex than the restraint of self-destructive impulses or isolated gestures of protest. The freedom of the prisoner, whether it is granted in the name of humanity, economic efficiency, or reformation, and limited though it may be, creates a situation in which crimes among inmates are possible. Theft, murder, fraud, sodomy—all exist as possible acts of deviance within the prison and the custodians have the duty of preventing them from being converted into realities. As in the case of custody, however, difficulties arise at two points. First there is the question of the specific measures which must be taken to insure the maintenance of order; and second there is the question of the value or priority to be attached to the maintenance of order as opposed to possibly competing objectives. If extensive regulations, constant surveillance, and swift reprisals are used, prison officials are likely to run headlong into the supporters of reform who argue that such procedures are basically inimical to the doctor-patient relationship which should serve as the model for therapy.

Finally, there is the question of just what should be done to reform the captive criminal. Of all the tasks which the prison is called upon to perform, none is more ambiguous than the task of changing criminals into noncriminals. The goal itself is far from clear and even when agreement can be reached on this point, as we have mentioned before, the means to achieve it remain uncertain.

The administrator of the maximum security prison, then, finds himself confronted with a set of social expectations which pose numerous dilemmas when an attempt is made to

17

translate them into a concrete, rational policy. Somehow he must resolve the claims that the prison should exact vengeance, erect a specter to terrify the actual or potential deviant, isolate the known offender from the free community, and effect a change in the personality of his captives so that they gladly follow the dictates of the law—and in addition maintain order within his society of prisoners and see that they are employed at useful labor. If the policy of the prison sometimes seems to exhibit a certain inconsistency, we might do well to look at the inconsistency of the philosophical setting in which the prison rests. In any event, let us examine the resolution of these problems as they are expressed in the regime which the officials of the New Jersey State Maximum Security Prison attempt to impose on their captives.

III

The Task of Custody

There seems little doubt that the task of custody looms largest in the eyes of the officials of the New Jersey State Prison and in this they differ but little from most if not all of the administrators who are charged with the responsibility for maximum security institutions in the United States. The prison exists as a dramatic symbol of society's desire to segregate the criminal, whatever reasons may lie behind that desire; and the prison wall, that line between the pure and impure, has all the emotional overtones of a woman's maidenhead. One escape from the maximum security prison is sufficient to arouse public opinion to a fever pitch and an organization which stands or falls on a single case moves with understandable caution. The officials, in short, know on which side their bread is buttered. Their continued employment is tied up with the successful performance of custody and if society is not sure of the priority to be attached to the tasks assigned the prison, the overriding importance of custody is perfectly clear to the officials.

If the wall and its guards were sufficient to prevent escapes, the task of custody in the New Jersey State Prison would be made relatively simple. In fact, however, these barriers are effective only because of a wide variety of security measures which must be carried out deep within the prison itself. The 20-foot climb and the pointing guns are hazards, but they are not insurmountable if the prisoner can effect a happy juxtaposition of materials, time, place, and events. A ladder constructed of dental floss which can be hidden in the palm of one hand; a fight in another part of the prison to serve as a momentary diversion; the prisoner waiting in the exercise yard for the welcome cover of darkness; a prison uniform stripped of its distinguishing marks to serve as civilian dress—these are the preparations for escape which must be detected long before the final dash for freedom occurs. To the prison officials, then, the guards on the wall form the last line of the institution's defenses, not the first, and they fight their battle at the center of their position rather than at its perimeter.

But are the custodians and their captives really locked in such combat? Is there a touch of something akin to paranoia in the ceaseless precautions of the officials? Certainly there is no convincing proof that the majority of the imprisoned criminals are bent on flight. In fact, the prison officials are convinced that only a few restraints are needed to persuade many of their prisoners from attempting to escape. The officials are aware that there are psychological walls surrounding their community—such as the threat of being a hunted man or the imminence of parole—which are more powerful than those of stone for many men. Nearly 55 percent of the inmates in the institution can look forward to being released within two years after their arrival and 85 percent will be discharged within four years; a precarious freedom won by a dangerous escape may make the game seem hardly worth the candle. Yet at the same time the officials of the prison are convinced that *some* inmates—an unknown number— will seize the slightest opportunity to break out of the institution and that in dealing with these men a moment's inattention is an invitation to disaster. Since hardly a year goes by

19

without the detection of an attempted escape, the suspicions of the officials are far from groundless. The plan may be discovered in its earlier phase—as when a half-finished tunnel was found under the floor of an industrial shop—or aborted only at the last moment—as when a prisoner was killed by the guards on top of the laundry after he had escaped from the death house where he awaited his execution in the electric chair. But whether uncovered soon or late, the attempts to escape occur with sufficient frequency to persuade the officials that their security measures are not the foolish gestures of an old woman looking under the bed for the thief who is never there.

Unfortunately, the prison officials can predict only in the grossest fashion *which* of their captives will try to elude them, however certain they may be that some will do so. It is true that there are a few prisoners who can clearly be labelled "security risks"—men so intransigent in their dislike of imprisonment that no plot is too daring, no risk too great, if the goal is freedom. These are the *escape artists* in the argot of the inmates and in another social situation (a prisoner-of-war camp for example) such men often serve as symbols of indomitable courage. But the guards of New Jersey State Prison can rarely allow themselves the luxury of abstracting personal qualities from the context in which they are exhibited. The few criminals who will certainly try to escape are simply viewed as the identifiable nucleus of a larger, ill-defined body of rash prisoners who might attempt to escape under favorable circumstances. The custodians, then, face a population of prisoners requiring various degrees of surveillance and control, ranging from the utmost vigilance to perhaps none at all. Their difficulty is that with the exception of a handful of *escape artists* they have no dependable way of distinguishing the requirements of one man from another. In the light of the public uproar which follows close on the heels of an escape from prison, it is not surprising that the prison officials have chosen the course of treating all inmates as if they were equally serious threats to the task of custody;

stringent security measures are imposed on the entire inmate population with the full realization that much of the effort may be unnecessary.

Searching cells for contraband material; repeatedly counting all inmates to insure that each man is in his appointed place; censoring mail for evidence of escape plans; inspecting bars, windows, gratings, and other possible escape routes—all are obvious precautions. The custodians, however, do not stop with these, for they have found to their bitter knowledge that in a maximum security prison the most innocent-appearing activity may be a symptom of a major breach in the institution's defenses. Pepper stolen from the mess-hall may be used as a weapon, to be thrown in the eyes of a guard during a bid for freedom. A prisoner growing a moustache may be acquiring a disguise to help him elude the police once he has gotten on the other side of the wall. Extra electrical fixtures in a cell can cause a blown fuse in a moment of crisis. A fresh coat of paint in a cell may be used by an industrious prisoner to cover up his handiwork when he has cut the bars and replaced the filings with putty.

All of these seemingly innocent acts and many more like them are prohibited, therefore, by the regulations of the prison. If it is argued that such security measures are based on relatively rare events, the officials can only agree. They will add, however, that prisoners are ingenious in devising ways to escape and it is the duty of the officials to prevent escapes from occurring. If it is argued that the elaborate system of regulations which is established in the name of custody must prove irksome to the prisoner who has never contemplated escape—well, the Army has a classic expression for such situations.

The Task of Internal Order

If custody is elevated to the first rank in the list of tasks to be accomplished by the prison, the objective of maintaining internal order is a close second. And it must be admitted that under the best of circumstances the maintenance of order

21

among a group of men such as those who are confined in the New Jersey State Prison would present formidable problems. A committee appointed by Governor Alfred E. Driscoll in 1952 to investigate the prison noted that the institution has long served as a dumping ground or catch basin for the state's entire correctional system; and in their report the committee stated that ". . . the inmate population of Trenton Prison included, in addition to the 'ordinary' prisoners who constitute the majority of the population, insane and near-insane, mental defectives, unstable psychopaths, some of them highly assaultive, prisoners convicted as sexual psychopaths, passive homosexuals, aggressive 'wolves' with long records of fights and stabbings, escape artists, agitators, and 'incorrigibles' of all ages."[5]

Whatever may be the personal traits possessed by these men which helped bring them to the institution, it is certain that the conditions of prison life itself create strong pressures pointed toward behavior defined as criminal in the free community. Subjected to prolonged material deprivation, lacking heterosexual relationships, and rubbed raw by the irritants of life under compression, the inmate population is pushed in the direction of deviation from, rather than adherence to, the legal norms. The nature and the consequences of the deprivations and frustrations of existence in the custodial institution will be a major concern in later chapters; at this point it is enough to point out that the custodians' task of maintaining order within the prison is acerbated by the conditions of life which it is their duty to impose on their captives. The prison official, then, is caught up in a vicious circle where he must suppress the very activity that he helps cause. It is not surprising that he should overlook his part in the process, that he should tend to view the prisoner as innately vicious or depraved. The conduct of the inmate is used to justify further repressive measures and the antagonisms between the guard and his prisoner spiral upward.

[5] New Jersey Committee to Examine and Investigate the Prison and Parole Systems of New Jersey, *Report*, November 21, 1952.

In addition to their responsibility for enforcing the laws of the free community (such as the prohibitions against murder, assault, theft, homosexuality, etc.), the custodians demand, obedience to an extensive body of regulations peculiar to the prison alone. Many of these rules are theoretically intended to curb behavior which might endanger custody, but there remains a set of regulations intended to promote "quiet," "peaceful," or "orderly" relationships within the New Jersey State Prison, according to the custodians. When we examine these rules we cannot help but be struck by their apparent pettiness and perhaps a few illustrations will make my point clear. The following are taken from the *Handbook for Inmates*, issued to each prisoner on his arrival:

When the bell rings for meals, work, or other assignment, turn out your light, see that your water is turned off, and step out of your cell promptly.

Form by twos when passing through the Center. Keep your place in line unless you are ordered to step out.

When walking in line maintain a good posture. Face forward and keep your hands out of your pockets.

On returning to your Wing, go directly to your cell, open the door, step in, and close the door without slamming it.

Gambling in any form is not allowed.

Do not speak or make any gestures to persons who are visiting the institution.

Such regimentation has long been a focus of attack for the critics of penal institutions and a number of writers would argue, along with the authors of a recent textbook on criminology, that "many such asinine injunctions could be eliminated immediately."[6] Certainly a regime which involves such detailed regulations is distasteful from the viewpoint of democratic values, but before we condemn the prison officials as oppressors, who allow rules to grow through sheer stupidity

[6] Harry Elmer Barnes and Negley K. Teeters, *New Horizons in Criminology*, New York: Prentice-Hall, Inc., 1952, pp. 438-439.

23

or a willful disregard for man's dignity, let us examine their position.

First, there is the question of the nature and extent of the disorder which would arise within the prison if the custodians did not exercise strict supervision and control over the activities of the inmates. There are few who will claim that in the complete absence of supervision and control the inmate population would live harmoniously within the walls of their prison. Rather, criticism has been directed against the apparent triviality of many regulations which seem to have no other purpose than the domination of the prisoner for the sake of domination alone. Why, for example, must inmates pass two by two through the Center? Why must inmates go directly to their cells on returning to the Wing? The answer of the custodians is plain: They are few and the inmates are many. A moment's escape from surveillance provides the prisoner with an opportunity to perform a variety of serious illegal acts. What is innocent now may prove dangerous later—as when a route of exchange for cigarettes becomes a route of exchange for weapons. Gambling may lead to unpaid debts, unpaid debts may lead to a knifing. In brief, say the custodians, the maximum security prison is not a Boy Scout camp and do not ask us to treat it as if it were. We are dealing with men inured to violence and other forms of anti-social behavior and order can be maintained only if we establish rules which eliminate the situations in which such behavior can arise.

Second, there is the question of the value of order within the prison as opposed to the value of the individual's freedom from rigid supervision and control. In this matter the New Jersey State Prison differs sharply from the free community which rarely prohibits acts that *may* lead to harmful consequences. Outside the walls a certain amount of harmful or illegal behavior is taken as the inevitable and, in a sense, acceptable consequence of individual freedom. The social cost of eliminating deviance or reducing deviance to a minimum is held to be greater than the social cost of the deviance itself. In the prison, however, a different calculation is at work

24

—the assurance of order is regarded as worth the price paid in terms of the inmate's subjugation to detailed regulations. The reason for this critical reversal of values is much the same as in the case of custody: Public reactions to "disturbances" within the prison make it abundantly clear that such events are to be avoided at all costs.

It is quite possible that the custodians overestimate the amount of disorder which would occur in the absence of rigid controls reaching far into what seem to be irrelevant areas of life. And, possibly, the price paid for eliminating disorder is far too high. One is a question of fact and the other is a question of value, but the prison official is neither a scientist free to experiment nor a philosopher. In the regime of the custodians of the New Jersey State Maximum Security Prison, the dilemma between a permissive social atmosphere and internal order has been resolved in favor of the latter.

The Task of Self-Maintenance

In giving precedence to the tasks of custody and the maintenance of order, the officials of the New Jersey State Prison move in the direction of ever greater control of their captives. The prisoner is, in a sense, sacrificed to these objectives and the prevention of escapes and disturbances within the walls is purchased by means of the inmate's autonomy. There are only a few to mourn his loss and if the prisoner himself complains, he is apt to be ignored on the grounds that a man who has committed a crime has given up the rights of the free individual. He is, after all, it is said, a man who is supposed to be undergoing punishment and it is argued that a permissive or supportive atmosphere for the prisoner—demanded on the grounds of reformation or humanitarianism—must be forfeited for more important concerns. When it comes to the issue of penal labor, however, the custodians face a knottier problem. The efficient use of inmate labor in the production of goods and services also requires a more permissive or supportive atmosphere for the prisoner, if only in the sense that some attention must be paid to the opinions, at-

25

titudes, and desires of the inmate in order to motivate him to work. And the efficient use of inmate labor is not thrust aside without serious repercussions.

Now it is true that the New Jersey State Prison does not produce goods or services for the market which are equal in value to the cost of the institution's operation; a variety of social and economic interests prohibit the products of prison labor from entering into direct competition with those of private enterprise.[7] And although the prison does manufacture articles (such as automobile license tags, clothing, office furniture, etc.) for the use of other institutions and agencies of the state, the value of these products is far less than the sum required to support the prison. None the less, the production of goods for use by the state in these so-called State-Use industries is an important gesture in the direction of a self-sustaining community in terms of labor: Approximately one half of the inmates are thus employed. In addition, the inmate population is required to perform the many details of institutional housekeeping, as we have mentioned before. As in every society, there are some men who cannot work and some men for whom no work can be found, together comprising a group—known as the Idle Men—approximately 300 in number. But the great majority of prisoners are employed in a variety of occupations in an enforced mimicry of the free community. The following presents a typical picture of work assignments in the New Jersey State Prison:

Work Assignment	Number of Inmates
Bakers	16
Band	18
Barbers	11
Center Runners	3
Photographers	2
Commissary Department	66
Engineer Department	1
Garage	6
Hospital Department	34
Ice Plant	3

[7] See footnote 4, page 16.

Work Assignment	Number of Inmates
Industrial Office	6
Industrial Store Room	4
Inmates' Store	3
Laundry	19
Prison Store Room	21
Receiving Gate	2
Repair Department	52
Runners and Helpers	66
School and Library	6
Shipping Platform	4
Print Shop	23
Shoe Shop	41
Machine Shop	15
Tailor Shop	108
Tag Shop	60
Woodworking Shop	25
Utility Gang	12
Outside Store Room	3
Trucks	3
Officers' Personal Service	11
Yard Gang	22
Swill Platform	3
Inside Sanitary Detail	3
Front House Cleaners	4
Upholstery Shop	27
Not Capable of Working	40
Unemployed	203
In Quarantine	55
Sick in Hospital	25

Whether prisoners labor as a duty, a privilege, an economic necessity, or as a cure, the fact that custodians and inmates are caught up in the complex of work has profound implications for the nature of imprisonment. In the first place, if inmates work they must have some freedom of movement and this provides an opportunity for interaction which would otherwise be lacking. In the second place, tools and materials must be provided, thus greatly broadening the resource base of this society of captives, if somehow the stream of goods flowing into the prison can be deflected from its legitimate channel. Unlike a community living in a harsh physical environment where no effort can overcome the stinginess of nature, the prisoners live in an environment made harsh by man-made decrees and only officialdom stands interposed between the inmates and many of the amenities of life as represented by institutional supplies. In the third place (and this is perhaps the most important of all) the fact that prisoners work carries with it the implication that the prison produces, that there is some result for the thousands of man-hours expended each day. To a large extent the prison officials are held responsible for the output of the inmates and thus the custodians are drawn willy-nilly into the problems of an economic enterprise. The custodians cannot remain simply custodians, content to search a cell for contraband or to censor the mail; now they must manage men as well.[8]

To get prisoners to work is, however, a far different matter from preventing escapes or maintaining internal order. It is true that if prisoners refuse to work they can be placed in solitary confinement or deprived of a variety of privileges. And since an inmate's sentence is reduced by one day for each five days that he works, a refusal to work can lead to a loss of this so-called Work Time.[9] These threats in the background appear to be sufficient to convince most of the inmate population that an outright refusal to work is unwise, but at the same time they appear to be incapable of preventing more subtle forms of rebellion. Apathy, sabotage, and the show of effort rather than the substance—the traditional answers of the slave—rise in the prison to plague the custodian-manager and his limited means of coercion cannot prevent them from occurring.[10]

[8] The task of organizing the labor of prisoners is shared with the officials in charge of State-Use Industries but the custodians must still be viewed as deeply enmeshed in a managerial role.

[9] The law of New Jersey stipulates that each prisoner may reduce the sentence he receives from the court by (a) earning one day per week for performing work assignments conscientiously (Work Time); and (b) earning commutation of his sentence, up to 60 days during the first year of imprisonment and in increasing amounts for subsequent years, for orderly deportment and manifest efforts at self-control and improvement (Good Time). Cf. New Jersey Department of Institutions and Agencies, Research Bulletin No. 18 "Two Thousand State Prisoners in New Jersey," Trenton, New Jersey, May 1954.

[10] The prison officials are prohibited by law from physically forcing an

The inability of the prison officials to elicit *conscientious* performance from their captives is not due simply to the fact that theirs is an involuntary labor force, a group of men who have been recruited unwillingly and in whom a residual hostility remains. Of equal or greater importance is the fact that incentives for the prisoner are almost completely lacking within the context of captivity. The wages of the inmate are fixed by the State Board of Control within a range of 10 cents to 35 cents per day, depending on his assignment, and this munificence is hardly calculated to stir the inmate to heights of effort. The monotonous, unskilled nature of most jobs in the prison provides little intrinsic work satisfaction and the incentive of Work Time, like retirement benefits and other distant rewards of the free community, presents many drawbacks as a motivating force for here and now. There exists no hierarchy of power and responsibilities in the inmate labor force, since guards or civilian work supervisors exercise all supervision and control, thus eliminating the bait of promotion. Praise and recognition from the custodians for work well done have little value for the criminal in prison and the zealous prisoner must face the gibes and aggression of his fellow captives.

In attempting, then, to organize the inmate population into an efficient or conscientious working force—as opposed let us say, to a group of men who appear on the job and go through the motions—the custodians of the maximum security prison are confronted with a set of relatively unique administrative problems. The custodians, it is true, can push their prisoners into the semblance of work but beyond this point they move with difficulty. Unlike the masters of a concentration camp, the prison officials are barred from using extreme penalties, such as brute force or starvation, to extract high

---

inmate to work. In order to prevent inmates from refusing to work one day and agreeing to work the next (which might lead to serious disruptions in the scheduling of work activities) the officials have established a rule which asserts that any inmate who refuses to work must remain among the Idle Men for six months. Thus a refusal to work does not win a day of leisure to be traded for a fractional extension of one's sentence; rather, it entails a serious loss of Work Time and a prolonged period of enforced inactivity.

levels of effort. Unlike the managers of an industrial enterprise in the free community, they are denied the use of the common rewards of work incentives, such as meaningful monetary rewards or symbolic forms of recognition. The result tends to be a minimum of effort on the part of the prisoner—a form of inefficiency which is economically feasible only because the production of goods and services in the prison is but loosely linked to the discipline of the open market. Prisoners must be provided for, regardless of whether or not their own efforts are sufficient to win the means of subsistence. If the value of their work is small, they will be little affected, as long as they do not openly rebel. If the value of their work is large, they have no reason to look forward to increased benefits. The custodians, however, do not enjoy such a tolerance and they must pay attention to the output of the prison even if the prisoners do not; it is true that the prison will not go out of business, but the custodians may very well find themselves replaced.

In short, the officials of the New Jersey State Prison find themselves in the uncomfortable position of needing the labor of their captives far more than do the captives themselves; and at the same time the officials prohibit (and are prohibited from) the use of effective rewards and punishments to secure conscientious performance. When we add the burdens of security and internal order which make the simplest job cumbersome, through the need for surveillance and control, it is not surprising that the custodians find the task of making the prison an approximation of a self-sustaining community both difficult and discouraging.[11] With too many men for too few jobs, ham-strung by worn-out and outmoded machinery, lacking an adequate budget, under pressure from economic inter-

[11] The tasks of preventing escapes and maintaining internal order pose many problems for the efficient organization of work beyond those encountered on the job itself. The classification committee—which gives out work assignments within the prison—cannot afford to fill vacant jobs on the basis of the skills and experience of prisoners. Instead, they must pay primary attention to the opportunities offered by a particular job for "getting into trouble" and an inmate's record for violence, homosexuality, alcoholism, etc.

30

ests in the free community, and hampered by their own commitment to competing objectives, the officials of the New Jersey State Prison are in an unenviable position. It is in this light that we must interpret the scene encountered so often in the prison—a group of five or six inmates conversing or sleeping in the corner of an industrial shop or in a storeroom, unmolested by their guard. If the scene is a parody of the stereotype of penal servitude, it is the prisoners and not the custodians who find the situation humorous.

The Task of Punishment

It is sometimes said that criminals are placed in prison not *for* punishment but *as* punishment;[12] presumably, stress is being placed on the idea that the officials of the custodial institution are determined not to hurt their captives either physically or mentally beyond the pain involved in confinement itself. And, in a certain sense, it would certainly appear to be true that the administrators of the New Jersey State Prison have no great interest in inflicting punishments on their prisoners for the crimes which they committed in the free community, as paradoxical as it may seem. There is no indication in the day-to-day operation of the prison that the officials have any desire to act as avenging angels; nor do the officials exhibit much attachment to the idea that a painful period of imprisonment is likely to deter the criminal who has been confined—the reappearance of discharged prisoners has made them grow cynical on that score.

It is true that punishing physical conditions are still inflicted on the prisoners to some extent, for as late as 1952 the committee to investigate the New Jersey State Prison could report that ". . . the prison buildings are in the bad condition that one would expect from their age. . . . Proper sanitary standards are difficult to maintain. Among the prisoner's complaints were that rats infest the buildings of the prison, that sewer gas escapes from the service tunnel between

12 See Sanford Bates, *Prisons and Beyond*, New York: The Macmillan Company, 1936.

31

the cells . . . and that sanitary conditions are generally bad."[13] And it is true that isolated acts of brutality on the part of the guards still occur. But the gross sadism and systematic neglect which aroused the anger of John Howard and similar critics of prisons have largely disappeared in the United States today with a few notable exceptions; and the New Jersey State Prison follows not the exceptions but the general rule.

Yet if the custodians are not motivated by a desire to inflict punishments, how are the many deprivations imposed on the inmates to be explained? Why, for example, are prisoners permitted to spend only twenty-five dollars each month at the inmate store for items such as tobacco, candy, soap, and so on? Why is so-called hobby work sharply curtailed? Why is the number of visits and letters from the outside world which are allowed the prisoner so small? These, indeed, are the questions raised by the inmates themselves and they believe they know the true answer: The officials wish to punish the prisoner but they cannot openly admit it. The claim of the officials that the many restrictions, the many punishing features of prison life, are inflicted in the name of custody and internal order is simply viewed as a rationalization. The "basic" motive of the officials, according to many inmates (and to many critics of the penal system as well), is hatred of the confined criminal and it is this which determines the nature of the custodians' regime.

Now we have argued before that a punitive orientation toward the criminal does exist in society and that this orientation is reflected in the conditions of prison life. And it is certainly true that many prison officials believe that, in general, criminals should be punished. But to say that a desire for retribution is the basic or primary motive of the officials as they go about their daily routines is quite another thing. In fact, it would appear to be at least equally valid to claim that the maintenance of a quiet, orderly, peaceful institution is the dominant desire of the custodians and that the past

[13] New Jersey Committee to Examine and Investigate the Prison and Parole Systems of New Jersey, *Report*, November 21, 1952.

criminality of the prisoner serves as a justification for the stringent controls which are imposed to achieve this end. The objective of eliminating incidents is not a rationalization for inflicting deprivations on the criminal within the walls; *rather, the reverse is true and the prior deviance of the prisoner is a rationalization for using such extreme measures to avoid any events which would excite public indignation.*

In any case, the officials of the New Jersey State Prison rarely turn to the behavior of the captive before he entered the institution as something for which atonement must be secured. In reality, much of the officials' activity is defined not as punishing but as providing adequate food, housing, medical care, etc., for the society of captives which is their responsibility. Of course, it could be argued that these and similar measures to maintain a decent standard of living or adequate standard of care are merely additional weapons for the custodians in their task of maintaining an orderly institution. The threat of reducing the standard—of placing a man in solitary confinement, restricting his diet, or withdrawing recreational and visiting privileges—can be viewed merely as a mechanism of control in dealing with men who are already being punished near the limits set by society. There is undoubtedly some truth in this, as we shall see shortly, and it is certainly not a simple fondness for the prisoner which drives the custodians of the New Jersey State Prison to take such an interest in his well-being. At the same time to view provisions for the inmate's welfare as nothing more than a manipulative attempt to grant privileges which can later be taken away is to ignore a fundamental link which exists between the captors and their captives. Guards and prisoners are drawn from the same culture and they hold many of the same values and beliefs. They share a common language and a common historical experience. They may stand opposed across the chasm which separates the convicted felon and the law-abiding citizen or the perhaps even greater chasm which divides the ruler and the ruled. But the criminal in the maximum security prison today is not defined as an individual who has been stripped of his humanity and it is this fact which does much to temper the totalitarian power system of the prison.

The Task of Reform

If the officials of the New Jersey State Prison are relatively indifferent when it comes to punishing their prisoners for their past sins, so also are they relatively indifferent when it comes to saving their prisoners from sins in the future. It is true that there is frequent mention of "individualization of treatment," "correction," "self-discipline," "a favorable change in attitudes," and so on, by the Department of Institutions and Agencies.[14] And it is true that within the prison itself a number of counsellors, a chaplain, a psychologist, and several teachers for the inmate school have the duty of somehow implanting that inner conviction in the offender which will keep him from the path of crime when he is released. But allegiance to the goal of rehabilitation tends to remain at the verbal level, an expression of hope for public consumption rather than a coherent program with an integrated, professional staff.

There are some writers, of course, who claim that any attempts to rehabilitate the offender in prison are futile. Some argue that the causes of criminal behavior do not lie within the individual himself, but in the social environment, in the form of slums, poverty, underworld associates, etc. Since the prison experience does not and cannot touch these, imprissonment is a waste of time as far as reformation is concerned; and to place an individual in custody for breaking the law is as foolish as locking up a dollar bill because it has lost its purchasing power. Others argue that the causes of crime are to be found deep in the individual's unconscious mind. Prison officials are not equipped by either training or experience to eradicate these causes and in any case the authoritarian, custodian-prisoner relationship is enough to warp the soul

[14] See, for example, New Jersey Department of Institutions and Agencies Research Bulletin No. 111, November 1953.

of the innocent, let alone the guilty. The officials of the New Jersey State Prison do not, in general, accept such pessimistic arguments, but at the same time they are far from sanguine about their ability to rehabilitate the offender. In fact, in so far as reform of the prisoner is seriously considered as a basis for the formation of administrative policy, the officials tend to take a position which is a complex mixture of faith and cynicism: Imprisonment is very likely to be defined as a success if only it does not make the offender worse. If progress is impossible, then one should at least fight against retreat.

In many of the custodial institutions in the United States today, this view of the task of reform as a holding action finds expression as an attempt to avoid the more corrosive abnormalities of prison existence. Provisions for medical care, recreation, schooling, library facilities, visiting privileges—all, it is held, make the prison less of a prison, and imitation of the free community may be justified not only on humanitarian grounds but also on the grounds of its possible effects on the criminal's behavior after he has left the prison. Since there is no valid test of the individual's criminal proclivities, no one can say with assurance that a given custodial regime has led a prisoner backward, forward, or left him untouched; and prison officials are free to pursue their hope that imitation of the free community at least does no harm and perhaps may do some good.

However, under the rule of the Warden of the New Jersey State Prison at the time of this study, the idea that the confined criminal can at least be prevented from deteriorating, if he cannot be cured, has taken a somewhat different turn. With wide experience in the administration of penal institutions and with professional training in the social sciences, the Warden has hammered out a philosophy of custody in which the prevention of deviant behavior among inmates while in prison is the most potent device for preparing the prisoner to follow the dictates of society when he is released. Education, recreation, counselling, and other measures designed to lessen the oppressiveness of prison life assume a relatively

35

minor position compared to a system of control which attempts to make the prisoner learn compliance to duly constituted authority. It is important to examine his views at some length, for the maximum security prison, like every organization, bears the mark of the particular men in power. The following statement appears in the Warden's report on the operations of the New Jersey State Prison for the year 1953-1954:

Custody is frequently dismissed as a rather sordid and punitive operation, consisting chiefly of keeping inmates perpetually locked, counted, and controlled. Almost as if in opposition to this, treatment and welfare are described as attempts to introduce freedom and dignity into custody's restrictive, punitive context by the provision of recreation, education, and counselling. This traditional contrast, disfigured by bias and half-truth, misses the central reality of the inmate's life in prison.

The reality is simply this: The welfare of the individual inmate, to say nothing of his psychological freedom and dignity, does not importantly depend on how much education, recreation, and consultation he receives but rather depends on how he manages to live and relate with other inmates who constitute his crucial and only meaningful world. It is what he experiences in this world; how he attains satisfactions from it, how he avoids its pernicious effects—how, in a word, he survives in it that determines his adjustment and decides whether he will emerge from prison with an intact or shattered integrity. The significant impact of institutional officials is therefore not in terms of their relations with the inmate alone, but in terms of a total effect on the social world in which he is inextricably enmeshed. In these terms, an evaluation of the institution's contribution to the welfare of its inmates may not realistically be made with the typical institutional platitudes and statistics about hours of recreation, treatment, and education. The evaluation must rather be made in terms of how the prison authorities are affecting the total social climate, how successful they are in enabling the less hostile persons to advance themselves, how successfully they are protecting these people from intimidation or exploitation by the more antisocial inmates, how effectively they curb and frustrate the lying, swindling, and covert violence which is always under the surface of the inmate social world.

The efficient custodian now emerges from the role of restrictor and becomes the one who safeguards inmate welfare. Most in-

36

mates will admit and even require the keepers to assume this function. They understand that the metal detector which un-covers a file intended for an escape attempt will also detect a knife intended for the unsuspecting back of a friend. Inmates will privately express their relief at the construction of a segrega-tion wing which protects them from the depredations of men who are outlaws even in the prison world. Much as they complain of the disciplinary court which punishes them for their infractions, they are grateful for the swift and stern justice meted out to in-mates who loot their cells. In short, these men realize, sometimes dimly, sometimes keenly, that a control system which is lax enough to permit thievery and intimidation must eventually result in a deterioration and vicious circle.

I have suggested previously that such an argument might be viewed simply as a rationalization for the totalitarian re-gime of the custodians.[15] It might be claimed that this argu-ment is at best a guess, since we do not have definite proof that securing compliance with the regulations of the prison increases the individual's readiness to conform to the general normative demands of society when he is released. And it might be asserted that the argument is a valid one, not be-cause of hypothetical consequences for reform, but because strict control is necessary to create tolerable living conditions among hundreds of inmates confined in a small space. At this point, however, it is not the validity of the argument that is relevant for our analysis but its implications for the regime of the custodians. By viewing the enforcement of prison regula-tions as being more important for the rehabilitation of the criminal than education, recreation, consultation, etc., the Warden has reinforced the traditional low priority attached to the efforts of those charged with the task of reform. What-ever value might be attached to such a system of priorities, its meaning for the social structure of the prison is clear: It is the control of the prisoner's behavior which is stressed rather than the control of the prisoner's mind, on the grounds that if the individual's actions are forced to match normative de-

15 It should be noted that this report was written shortly after a number of serious riots when there was a pressing need to clarify the position of the custodial force and to bolster its morale.

mands, the mind will follow after. And in this respect the prison differs markedly from a number of systems of totalitarian power which seek to capture the emotional and intellectual allegiance of those who are ruled as well as their overt obedience. In the eyes of the officials of the New Jersey State Prison, the task of reform does not consist primarily of an ideological or psychological struggle in which an attempt is made to change the inmates' beliefs, attitudes, and goals. Instead, it consists largely of a battle for compliance. The officials of the prison, then, are indifferent to the task of reform, not in the sense that they reject reform out of hand as a legitimate organizational objective, but in the sense that rehabilitation tends to be seen as a theoretical, distant, and somewhat irrelevant by-product of successful performance at the tasks of custody and internal order. A released prisoner may or may not commit another crime in the free community, but that crude test of the prison's accomplishments in the area of reform lies far away. Within the walls, in the clear-cut scope of the custodian's responsibilities, the occurrence of escapes and disorders is a weightier concern.

IV

Emile Durkheim, Thurmond Arnold, Sir James Stephen, and many others have pointed out that the legal process serves as a highly dramatic method of affirming collective sentiments concerning the wrongness of criminal behavior. Norms, once implanted, do not thrive without replenishment and the punishment of the offender symbolizes anew the immorality of the deviant act.

Yet in a modern, complex society, the punishment of the offender has grown complex and we are no longer satisfied to stone the individual for his crime. We have created a social organization—the prison—which stands interposed between the law-abiding community and the offender. We have created new demands concerning how the offender should be handled and we have continually changed the limits within which the demands should be fulfilled. The result has been something of a jerry-built social structure, pieced together over the years and appealing to few. The custodians, however, can find little comfort in the conflicts and ambiguities of the free community's directives concerning the proper aims of imprisonment. They must somehow take these demands and these limited means and construct a regime—a social order—to which they hope they can make their captives conform. If the regime is a totalitarian one, it does not necessarily mean that the custodians believe that a society in which crime is checked by imposing rigid controls and deprivations is preferable to a society in which crime is checked by other means. Rather, it expresses in part our own lack of knowledge about how to better proceed; and, in part, it reflects the fact that when all else is said and done, society is still apt to attach the greatest importance to the prevention of escapes and disorders regardless of the cost.

The officials of the New Jersey State Maximum Security Prison, then, have designed a social order which should —in theory at least—minimize the possibility of escapes and disturbances within the walls. Self-maintenance and exacting retribution appear much farther down on the list of objectives and the task of reform is perhaps the lowest of all—unless, of course, securing adherence to prison regulations is in fact the best road to rehabilitation. But as we pointed out in the beginning of this chapter, this social order is not a reality but a statement of what *should* be. We must now examine what occurs in actuality.

CHAPTER THREE

THE DEFECTS OF TOTAL POWER

"FOR THE NEEDS of mass administration today," said Max Weber, "bureaucratic administration is completely indispensable. The choice is between bureaucracy and dilettantism in the field of administration."[1] To the officials of the New Jersey State Prison the choice is clear, as it is clear to the custodians of all maximum security prisons in the United States today. They are organized into a bureaucratic administrative staff—characterized by limited and specific rules, well-defined areas of competence and responsibility, impersonal standards of performance and promotion, and so on—which is similar in many respects to that of any modern, large-scale enterprise; and it is this staff which must see to the effective execution of the prison's routine procedures.

Of the approximately 300 employees of the New Jersey State Prison, more than two-thirds are directly concerned with the supervision and control of the inmate population. These form the so-called custodian force which is broken into three eight-hour shifts, each shift being arranged in a typical pyramid of authority. The day shift, however—on duty from 6:20 A.M. to 2:20 P.M.—is by far the largest. As in many organizations, the rhythm of life in the prison quickens with daybreak and trails off in the afternoon, and the period of greatest activity requires the largest number of administrative personnel.

In the bottom ranks are the Wing guards, the Tower

[1] Max Weber, *The Theory of Social and Economic Organization*, edited by Talcott Parsons, New York: Oxford University Press, 1947, p. 337.

guards, the guards assigned to the shops, and those with a miscellany of duties such as the guardianship of the receiving gate or the garage. Immediately above these men are a number of sergeants and lieutenants and these in turn are responsible to the Warden and his assistants.

The most striking fact about this bureaucracy of custodians is its unparalleled position of power—in formal terms, at least—vis-à-vis the body of men which it rules and from which it is supposed to extract compliance. The officials, after all, possess a monopoly on the legitimate means of coercion (or, as one prisoner has phrased it succinctly, "They have the guns and we don't"); and the officials can call on the armed might of the police and the National Guard in case of an overwhelming emergency. The 24-hour surveillance of the custodians represents the ultimate watchfulness and, presumably, noncompliance on the part of the inmates need not go long unchecked. The rulers of this society of captives nominally hold in their hands the sole right of granting rewards and inflicting punishments and it would seem that no prisoner could afford to ignore their demands for conformity. Centers of opposition in the inmate population—in the form of men recognized as leaders by fellow prisoners—can be neutralized through the use of solitary confinement or exile to other State institutions.[2] The custodians have the right not only to issue and administer the orders and regulations which are to guide the life of the prisoner, but also the right to detain, try, and punish any individual accused of disobedience—a merging of legislative, executive, and judicial functions which has long been regarded as the earmark of complete domination. The officials of the prison, in short, appear to be the possessors of almost infinite power within their realm; and, at least on the surface, the bureaucratic staff should experience no great difficulty in

[2] Just as the Deep South served as a dumping-ground for particularly troublesome slaves before the Civil War, so too can the county jail or mental hospital serve as a dumping-ground for the maximum security prison. Other institutions, however, are apt to regard the Trenton Prison in somewhat the same way, as the report of the Governor's committee to investigate the prison has indicated. *Supra* page 22.

converting their rules and regulations—their blueprint for behavior—into a reality.

It is true, of course, that the power position of the custodial bureaucracy is not truly infinite. The objectives which the officials pursue are not completely of their own choosing and the means which they can use to achieve their objectives are far from limitless. The custodians are not total despots, able to exercise power at whim, and thus they lack the essential mark of infinite power, the unchallenged right of being capricious in their rule. It is this last which distinguishes terror from government, infinite power from almost infinite power, and the distinction is an important one. Neither by right nor by intention are the officials of the New Jersey State Prison free from a system of norms and laws which curb their actions. But within these limitations the bureaucracy of the prison is organized around a grant of power which is without an equal in American society; and if the rulers of any social system could secure compliance with their rules and regulations—however sullen or unwilling—it might be expected that the officials of the maximum security prison would be able to do so.

When we examine the New Jersey State Prison, however, we find that this expectation is not borne out in actuality. Indeed, the glaring conclusion is that despite the guns and the surveillance, the searches and the precautions of the custodians, the actual behavior of the inmate population differs markedly from that which is called for by official commands and decrees. Violence, fraud, theft, aberrant sexual behavior —all are common-place occurrences in the daily round of institutional existence in spite of the fact that the maximum security prison is conceived of by society as the ultimate weapon for the control of the criminal and his deviant actions. Far from being omnipotent rulers who have crushed all signs of rebellion against their regime, the custodians are engaged in a continuous struggle to maintain order—and it is a struggle in which the custodians frequently fail. Offenses committed by one inmate against another occur often, as do offenses committed by inmates against the officials and their rules. And the number of undetected offenses is, by universal agreement of both officials and inmates, far larger than the number of offenses which are discovered.

Some hint of the custodial bureaucracy's skirmishes with the population of prisoners is provided by the records of the disciplinary court which has the task of adjudicating charges brought by guards against their captives for offenses taking place within the walls. The following is a typical listing for a one-week period:

CHARGE	DISPOSITION
1) Insolence and swearing while being interrogated	1) Continue in segregation
2) Threatening an inmate	2) Drop from job
3) Attempting to smuggle roll of tape into institution	3) 1 day in segregation with restricted diet
4) Possession of contraband	4) 30 days loss of privileges
5) Possession of pair of dice	5) 2 days in segregation with restricted diet
6) Insolence	6) Reprimand
7) Out of place	7) Drop from job. Refer to classification committee for reclassification
8) Possession of home-made knife, metal, and emery paper	8) 5 days in segregation with restricted diet
9) Suspicion of gambling or receiving bets	9) Drop from job and change Wing assignment
10) Out of place	10) 15 days loss of privileges
11) Possession of contraband	11) Reprimand
12) Creating disturbance in Wing	12) Continue in segregation
13) Swearing at an officer	13) Reprimand
14) Out of place	14) 15 days loss of privileges
15) Out of place	15) 15 days loss of privileges

Even more revealing, however, than this brief and somewhat enigmatic record are the so-called charge slips in which the guard is supposed to write out the derelictions of the prisoner in some detail. In the New Jersey State Prison, Charge Slips form an administrative residue of past conflicts between captors and captives and the following accounts are a fair sample:

This inmate threatened an officer's life. When I informed this inmate he was to stay in to see the Chief Deputy on his charge he told me if he did not go to the yard I would get a shiv in my back.   Signed: Officer A_____
Inmate X cursing an officer. In mess hall inmate refused to put excess bread back on tray. Then he threw the tray on the floor. In the Center, inmate cursed both Officer Y and myself.
                    Signed: Officer B_____
This inmate has been condemning everyone about him for going to work. The Center gave orders for him to go to work this A.M. which he refused to do. While searching his cell I found drawings of picks and locks.   Signed: Officer C_____
Fighting. As this inmate came to 1 Wing entrance to go to yard this A.M. he struck inmate G in the face.
                    Signed: Officer D_____
Having fermented beverage in his cell. Found while inmate was in yard.   Signed: Officer E_____
Attempting to instigate wing disturbance. When I asked him why he discarded [sic] my order to quiet down he said he was going to talk any time he wanted to and_____me and do whatever I wanted in regards to it.   Signed: Officer F_____
Possession of home-made shiv sharpened to razor edge on his person and possession of 2 more shivs in cell. When inmate was sent to 4 Wing officer H found 3″ steel blade in pocket. I ordered Officer M to search his cell and he found 2 more shivs in process of being sharpened.   Signed: Officer G_____
Insolence. Inmate objected to my looking at papers he was carrying in pockets while going to the yard. He snatched them violently from my hand and gave me some very abusive talk. This man told me to_____myself, and raised his hands as if to strike me. I grabbed him by the shirt and took him to the Center.
                    Signed: Officer H_____
Assault with knife on inmate K. During Idle Men's mess at approximately 11:10 A.M. this man assaulted Inmate K with a home-made knife. Inmate K was receiving his rations at the counter when Inmate B rushed up to him and plunged a knife in his chest, arm, and back. I grappled with him and with the assistance of Officers S and V, we disarmed the inmate and took him to the Center. Inmate K was immediately taken to the hospital.
                    Signed: Officer I_____

Sodomy. Found inmate W in cell with no clothing on and inmate Z on top of him with no clothing. Inmate W told me he was going to lie like a_____ _____ __ _____ to get out of it.
Signed: Officer J_____

Attempted escape on night of 4/15/53. This inmate along with inmates L and T succeeded in getting on roof of 6 Wing and having home-made bombs in their possession.
Signed: Officer K_____

Fighting and possession of home-made shiv. Struck first blow to Inmate P. He struck blow with a roll of black rubber rolled up in his fist. He then produced a knife made out of wire tied to a tooth brush.
Signed: Officer L_____

Refusing medication prescribed by Doctor W. Said "What do you think I am, a damn fool, taking that_____for a headache, give it to the doctor."
Signed: Officer M_____

Inmate loitering on tier. There is a clique of several men who lock on top tier, who ignore rule of returning directly to their cells and attempt to hang out on the tier in a group.
Signed: Officer N_____

It is hardly surprising that when the guards at the New Jersey State Prison were asked what topics should be of first importance in a proposed in-service training program, 98 percent picked "what to do in event of trouble." The critical issue for the moment, however, is that the dominant position of the custodial staff is more fiction than reality, if we think of domination as something more than the outward forms and symbols of power. If power is viewed as the probability that orders and regulations will be obeyed by a given group of individuals, as Max Weber has suggested,[3] the New Jersey State Prison is perhaps more notable for the doubtfulness of obedience than its certainty. The weekly records of the disciplinary court and Charge Slips provide an admittedly poor index of offenses or acts of noncompliance committed within the walls, for these form only a small, visible segment of an iceberg whose greatest bulk lies beneath the surface of official recognition. The public is periodically made aware of the officials' battle to enforce their regime within the prison, commonly in the form of allegations in the newspapers concerning homosexuality, illegal use of drugs, assaults, and so

3 *Ibid.*, p. 324.

on. But the ebb and flow of public attention given to these matters does not match the constancy of these problems for the prison officials who are all too well aware that "Incidents" —the very thing they try to minimize—are not isolated or rare events but are instead a commonplace. The number of "incidents" in the New Jersey State Prison is probably no greater than that to be found in most maximum security institutions in the United States and may, indeed, be smaller, although it is difficult to make comparisons. In any event, it seems clear that the custodians are bound to their captives in a relationship of conflict rather than compelled acquiescence, despite the custodians' theoretical supremacy, and we now need to see why this should be so.

II

In our examination of the forces which undermine the power position of the New Jersey State Prison's custodial bureaucracy, the most important fact is, perhaps, that the power of the custodians is not based on authority.

Now power based on authority is actually a complex social relationship in which an individual or a group of individuals is recognized as possessing a right to issue commands or regulations and those who receive these commands or regulations feel compelled to obey by a sense of duty. In its pure form, then, or as an ideal type, power based on authority has two essential elements: a rightful or legitimate effort to exercise control on the one hand and an inner, moral compulsion to obey, by those who are to be controlled, on the other. In reality, of course, the recognition of the legitimacy of efforts to exercise control may be qualified or partial and the sense of duty, as a motive for compliance, may be mixed with motives of fear or self-interest. But it is possible for theoretical purposes to think of power based on authority in its pure form and to use this as a baseline in describing the empirical case.[4]

---

[4] *Ibid.*, Introduction.

46

It is the second element of authority—the sense of duty as a motive for compliance—which supplies the secret strength of most social organizations. Orders and rules can be issued with the expectation that they will be obeyed without the necessity of demonstrating in each case that compliance will advance the subordinate's interests. Obedience or conformity springs from an internalized morality which transcends the personal feelings of the individual; the fact that an order or a rule is an order or a rule becomes the basis for modifying one's behavior, rather than a rational calculation of the advantages which might be gained.

In the prison, however, it is precisely this sense of duty which is lacking in the general inmate population. The regime of the custodians is expressed as a mass of commands and regulations passing down a hierarchy of power. In general, these efforts at control are regarded as legitimate by individuals in the hierarchy, and individuals tend to respond because they feel they "should," down to the level of the guard in the cellblock, the industrial shop, or the recreation yard.[5] But now these commands and regulations must jump a gap which separates the captors from the captives. And it is at this point that a sense of duty tends to disappear and with it goes that easily-won obedience which many organizations take for granted in the naïveté of their unrecognized strength. In the prison power must be based on something other than internalized morality and the custodians find themselves confronting men who must be forced, bribed, or cajoled into compliance. This is not to say that inmates feel that the efforts of prison officials to exercise control are wrongful or illegitimate; in general, prisoners do not feel that the prison officials have usurped positions of power which are not rightfully theirs, nor do prisoners feel that the orders and regulations which descend upon them from above represent an illegal extension of their rulers' grant of government. Rather, the noteworthy fact about the social system of the New Jersey State Prison

[5] Failures in this process within the custodial staff itself will be discussed in the latter portion of this chapter.

is that the bond between recognition of the legitimacy of control and the sense of duty has been torn apart. In these terms the social system of the prison is very similar to a *Gebietsverband*, a territorial group living under a regime imposed by a ruling few.[6] Like a province which has been conquered by force of arms, the community of prisoners has come to accept the validity of the regime constructed by their rulers but the subjugation is not complete. Whether he sees himself as caught by his own stupidity, the workings of chance, his inability to "fix" the case, or the superior skill of the police, the criminal in prison seldom denies the legitimacy of confinement.[7] At the same time, the recognition of the legitimacy of society's surrogates and their body of rules is not accompanied by an internalized obligation to obey and the prisoner thus accepts the fact of his captivity at one level and rejects it at another. If for no other reason, then, the custodial institution is valuable for a theory of human behavior because it makes us realize that men need not be motivated to conform to a regime which they define as rightful. It is in this apparent contradiction that we can see the first flaw in the custodial bureaucracy's assumed supremacy.

III

Since the Officials of prison possess a monopoly on the means of coercion, as we have pointed out earlier, it might be thought that the inmate population could simply be forced into conformity and that the lack of an inner moral compulsion to obey on the part of the inmates could be ignored. Yet the combination of a bureaucratic staff—that most modern,

---

[6] *Ibid.*, p. 149.

[7] This statement requires two qualifications. First, a number of inmates steadfastly maintain that they are innocent of the crime with which they are charged. It is the illegitimacy of their particular case, however, rather than the illegitimacy of confinement in general, which moves them to protest. Second, some of the more sophisticated prisoners argue that the conditions of imprisonment are wrong, although perhaps not illegitimate or illegal, on the grounds that reformation should be the major aim of imprisonment and the officials are not working hard enough in this direction.

rational form of mobilizing effort to exercise control—and the use of physical violence—that most ancient device to channel man's conduct—must strike us as an anomaly and with good reason. The use of force is actually grossly inefficient as a means for securing obedience, particularly when those who are to be controlled are called on to perform a task of any complexity. A blow with a club may check an immediate revolt, it is true, but it cannot assure effective performance on a punch-press. A "come-along," a straitjacket or a pair of handcuffs may serve to curb one rebellious prisoner in a crisis, but they will be of little aid in moving more than 1200 inmates through the messhall in a routine and orderly fashion. Furthermore, the custodians are well aware that violence once unleashed is not easily brought to heel and it is this awareness that lies behind the standing order that no guard should ever strike an inmate with his hand—he should always use a night stick. This rule is not an open invitation to brutality but an attempt to set a high threshold on the use of force in order to eliminate the casual cuffing which might explode into extensive and violent retaliation. Similarly, guards are under orders to throw their night sticks over the wall if they are on duty in the recreation yard when a riot develops. A guard without weapons, it is argued, is safer than a guard who tries to hold on to his symbol of office, for a mass of rebellious inmates may find a single night stick a goad rather than a restraint and the guard may find himself beaten to death with his own means of compelling order.

In short, the ability of the officials to physically coerce their captives into the paths of compliance is something of an illusion as far as the day-to-day activities of the prison are concerned and may be of doubtful value in moments of crisis. Intrinsically inefficient as a method of making men carry out a complex task, diminished in effectiveness by the realities of the guard-inmate ratio,[8] and always accompanied by the

---

[8] Since each shift is reduced in size by vacations, regular days off, sickness, etc., even the day shift—the largest of the three—can usually muster no more than 90 guards to confront the population of more than 1200 prisoners. The fact that they are so heavily out-numbered is not lost on the officials.

danger of touching off further violence, the use of physical force by the custodians has many limitations as a basis on which to found the routine operation of the prison. Coercive tactics may have some utility in checking blatant disobedience —if only a few men disobey. But if the great mass of criminals in prison are to be brought into the habit of conformity, it must be on other grounds. Unable to count on a sense of duty to motivate their captives to obey and unable to depend on the direct and immediate use of violence to insure a step-by-step submission to the rules, the custodians must fall back on a system of rewards and punishments.

Now if men are to be controlled by the use of rewards and punishments—by promises and threats—at least one point is patent: The rewards and punishments dangled in front of the individual must indeed be rewards and punishments from the point of view of the individual who is to be controlled. It is precisely on this point, however, that the custodians' system of rewards and punishments founders. In our discussion of the problems encountered in securing conscientious performance at work, we suggested that both the penalties and the incentives available to the officials were inadequate. This is also largely true, at a more general level, with regard to rewards and punishments for securing compliance with the wishes of the custodians in all areas of prison life.

In the first place, the punishments which the officials can inflict—for theft, assaults, escape attempts, gambling, insolence, homosexuality, and all the other deviations from the pattern of behavior called for by the regime of the custodians —do not represent a profound difference from the prisoner's usual status. It may be that when men are chronically deprived of liberty, material goods and services, recreational opportunities and so on, the few pleasures that are granted take on a new importance and the threat of their withdrawal is a more powerful motive for comformity than those of us in the free community can realize. To be locked up in the solitary confinement wing, that prison within a prison; to move from the monotonous, often badly prepared meals in the messhall to a diet of bread and water;[9] to be dropped from a dull, unsatisfying job and forced to remain in idleness—all, perhaps, may mean the difference between an existence which can be borne, painful though it may be, and one which cannot. But the officials of the New Jersey State Prison are dangerously close to the point where the stock of legitimate punishments has been exhausted and it would appear that for many prisoners the few punishments which are left have lost their potency. To this we must couple the important fact that such punishments as the custodians can inflict may lead to an increased prestige for the punished inmate in the eyes of his fellow prisoners. He may become a hero, a martyr, a man who has confronted his captors and dared them to do their worst. In the dialectics of the inmate population, punishments and rewards have, then, been reversed and the control measures of the officials may support disobedience rather than decrease it.

In the second place, the system of rewards and punishments in the prison is defective because the reward side of the picture has been largely stripped away. Mail and visiting privileges, recreational privileges, the supply of personal possessions—all are given to the inmate at the time of his arrival in one fixed sum. Even the so-called Good Time—the portion of the prisoner's sentence deducted for good behavior —is automatically subtracted from the prisoner's sentence when he begins his period of imprisonment.[10] Thus the officials have placed themselves in the peculiar position of granting the prisoner all available benefits or rewards at the time of his entrance into the system. The prisoner, then, finds himself unable to win any significant gains by means of compliance, for there are no gains left to be won.

From the viewpoint of the officials, of course, the privileges of the prison social system are regarded as rewards, as some-

---

[9] The usual inmate fare is both balanced and sufficient in quantity, but it has been pointed out that the meals are not apt to be particularly appetizing since prisoners must eat them with nothing but a spoon. Cf. Report of the Governor's Committee to Examine the Prison and Parole System of New Jersey, November 21, 1952, pp. 74-79.

[10] See footnote 9, page 28.

thing to be achieved. That is to say, the custodians hold that recreation, access to the inmate store, Good Time, or visits from individuals in the free community are conditional upon conformity or good behavior. But the evidence suggests that from the viewpoint of the inmates the variety of benefits granted by the custodians is not defined as something to be earned but as an inalienable right—as the just due of the inmate which should not turn on the question of obedience or disobedience within the walls. After all, the inmate population claims, these benefits have belonged to the prisoner from the time when he first came to the institution.

In short, the New Jersey State Prison makes an initial grant of all its rewards and then threatens to withdraw them if the prisoner does not conform. It does not start the prisoner from scratch and promise to grant its available rewards one by one as the prisoner proves himself through continued submission to the institutional regulations. As a result a subtle alchemy is set in motion whereby the inmates cease to see the rewards of the system as rewards, that is, as benefits contingent upon performance; instead, rewards are apt to be defined as obligations. Whatever justification might be offered for such a policy, it would appear to have a number of drawbacks as a method of motivating prisoners to fall into the posture of obedience. In effect, rewards and punishments of the officials have been collapsed into one and the prisoner moves in a world where there is no hope of progress but only the possibility of further punishments. Since the prisoner is already suffering from most of the punishments permitted by society, the threat of imposing those few remaining is all too likely to be a gesture of futility.

IV

Unable to depend on that inner moral compulsion or sense of duty which eases the problem of control in most social organizations, acutely aware that brute force is inadequate, and lacking an effective system of legitimate rewards and punishments which might induce prisoners to conform to institutional regulations on the grounds of self interest, the custodians of the New Jersey State Prison are considerably weakened in their attempts to impose their regime on their captive population. The result, in fact, is, as we have already indicated, a good deal of deviant behavior or noncompliance in a social system where the rulers at first glance seem to possess almost infinite power.

Yet systems of power may be defective for reasons other than the fact that those who are ruled do not feel the need to obey the orders and regulations descending on them from above. Systems of power may also fail because those who are supposed to rule are unwilling to do so. The unissued order, the deliberately ignored disobedience, the duty left unperformed—these are cracks in the monolith just as surely as are acts of defiance in the subject population. The "corruption" of the rulers may be far less dramatic than the insurrection of the ruled, for power unexercised is seldom as visible as power which is challenged, but the system of power still falters.[11]

Now the official in the lowest ranks of the custodial bureaucracy—the guard in the cellblock, the industrial shop, or the recreation yard—is the pivotal figure on which the custodial bureaucracy turns. It is he who must supervise and control the inmate population in concrete and detailed terms. It is he who must see to the translation of the custodial regime from blueprint to reality and engage in the specific battles for conformity. Counting prisoners, periodically reporting to the center of communications, signing passes, checking groups of inmates as they come and go, searching for contraband or signs of attempts to escape—these make up the minutiae of his eight-hour shift. In addition, he is supposed to be alert for violations of the prison rules which fall outside his routine sphere of surveillance. Not only must he detect and report deviant behavior after it occurs; he must curb deviant behavior before it arises as well as when he is called on to prevent a minor quarrel among prisoners from flaring into a more dan-

---

[11] Portions of the following discussion concerning the corruption of the guards' authority are to be found in Gresham M. Sykes, *Crime and Society*, New York: Random House, 1956.

gerous situation. And he must make sure that the inmates in his charge perform their assigned tasks with a reasonable degree of efficiency.

The expected role of the guard, then, is a complicated compound of policeman and foreman, of cadi, counsellor, and boss all rolled into one. But as the guard goes about his duties, piling one day on top of another (and the guard too, in a certain sense, is serving time in confinement), we find that the system of power in the prison is defective not only because the means of motivating the inmates to conform are largely lacking but also because the guard is frequently reluctant to enforce the full range of the institution's regulations. The guard frequently fails to report infractions of the rules which have occurred before his eyes. The guard often transmits forbidden information to inmates, such as plans for searching particular cells in a surprise raid for contraband. The guard often neglects elementary security requirements and on numerous occasions he will be found joining his prisoners in outspoken criticisms of the Warden and his assistants. In short, the guard frequently shows evidence of having been "corrupted" by the captive criminals over whom he stands in theoretical dominance. This failure within the ranks of the rulers is seldom to be attributed to outright bribery—bribery, indeed, is usually unnecessary, for far more effective influences are at work to bridge the gap supposedly separating captors and captives.

In the first place, the guard is in close and intimate association with his prisoners throughout the course of the working day. He can remain aloof only with great difficulty, for he possesses few of those devices which normally serve to maintain social distance between the rulers and the ruled. He cannot withdraw physically in symbolic affirmation of his superior position; he has no intermediaries to bear the brunt of resentment springing from orders which are disliked; and he cannot fall back on a dignity adhering to his office—he is a *hack* or a *screw* in the eyes of those he controls and an unwelcome display of officiousness evokes that great destroyer of unquestioned power, the ribald humor of the dispossessed.

There are many pressures in American culture to "be nice," to be a "good Joe," and the guard in the maximum security prison is not immune. The guard is constantly exposed to a sort of moral blackmail in which the first signs of condemnation, estrangement, or rigid adherence to the rules is countered by the inmates with the threat of ridicule or hostility. And in this complex interplay, the guard does not always start from a position of determined opposition to "being friendly." He holds an intermediate post in a bureaucratic structure between top prison officials—his captains, lieutenants, and sergeants—and the prisoners in his charge. Like many such figures, the guard is caught in a conflict of loyalties. He often has reason to resent the actions of his superior officers—the reprimands, the lack of ready appreciation, the incomprehensible order—and in the inmates he finds willing sympathizers: They too claim to suffer from the unreasonable irritants of power. Furthermore, the guard in many cases is marked by a basic ambivalence toward the criminals under his supervision and control. It is true that the inmates of the prison have been condemned by society through the agency of the courts, but some of these prisoners must be viewed as a success in terms of a worldly system of the values which accords high prestige to wealth and influence even though they may have been won by devious means; and the poorly paid guard may be gratified to associate with a famous racketeer. Moreover, this ambivalence in the guard's attitudes toward the criminals nominally under his thumb may be based on something more than a *sub rosa* respect for the notorious. There may also be a discrepancy between the judgments of society and the guard's own opinions as far as the "criminality" of the prisoner is concerned. It is difficult to define the man convicted of deserting his wife, gambling, or embezzlement as a desperate criminal to be suppressed at all costs and the crimes of even the most serious offenders lose their significance with the passage of time. In the eyes of the custodian, the in-

55

mate tends to become a man in prison rather than a criminal in prison and the relationship between captor and captive is subtly transformed in the process.

In the second place, the guard's position as a strict enforcer of the rules is undermined by the fact that he finds it almost impossible to avoid the claims of reciprocity. To a large extent the guard is dependent on inmates for the satisfactory performance of his duties; and like many individuals in positions of power, the guard is evaluated in terms of the conduct of the men he controls. A troublesome, noisy, dirty cellblock reflects on the guard's ability to "handle" prisoners and this ability forms an important component of the merit rating which is used as the basis for pay raises and promotions. As we have pointed out above, a guard cannot rely on the direct application of force to achieve compliance nor can he easily depend on threats of punishment. And if the guard does insist on constantly using the last few negative sanctions available to the institution—if the guard turns in Charge Slip after Charge Slip for every violation of the rules which he encounters—he becomes burdensome to the top officials of the prison bureaucratic staff who realize only too well that their apparent dominance rests on some degree of co-operation. A system of power which can enforce its rules only by bringing its formal machinery of accusation, trial, and punishment into play at every turn will soon be lost in a haze of pettifogging detail.

The guard, then, is under pressure to achieve a smoothly running tour of duty not with the stick but with the carrot, but here again his legitimate stock is limited. Facing demands from above that he achieve compliance and stalemated from below, he finds that one of the most meaningful rewards he can offer is to ignore certain offenses or make sure that he never places himself in a position where he will discover them. Thus the guard—backed by all the power of the State, close to armed men who will run to his aid, and aware that any prisoner who disobeys him can be punished if he presses charges against him—often discovers that his best path of action is to make "deals" or "trades" with the captives in his power. In effect, the guard buys compliance or obedience in certain areas at the cost of tolerating disobedience elsewhere.

Aside from winning compliance "where it counts" in the course of the normal day, the guard has another favor to be secured from the inmates which makes him willing to forego strict enforcement of all prison regulations. Many custodial institutions have experienced a riot in which the tables are turned momentarily and the captives hold sway over their quondam captors; and the rebellions of 1952 loom large in the memories of the officials of the New Jersey State Prison. The guard knows that he may some day be a hostage and that his life may turn on a settling of old accounts. A fund of good will becomes a valuable form of insurance and this fund is almost sure to be lacking if he has continually played the part of a martinet. In the folklore of the prison there are enough tales about strict guards who have had the misfortune of being captured and savagely beaten during a riot to raise doubts about the wisdom of demanding complete conformity.

In the third place, the theoretical dominance of the guard is undermined in actuality by the innocuous encroachment of the prisoner on the guard's duties. Making out reports, checking cells at the periodic count, locking and unlocking doors—in short, all the minor chores which the guard is called on to perform—may gradually be transferred into the hands of inmates whom the guard has come to trust. The cellblock runner, formally assigned the tasks of delivering mail, housekeeping duties, and so on, is of particular importance in this respect. Inmates in this position function in a manner analogous to that of the company clerk in the Armed Forces and like such figures they may wield power and influence far beyond the nominal definition of their role. For reasons of indifference, laziness, or naïveté, the guard may find that much of the power which he is supposed to exercise has slipped from his grasp.

Now power, like a woman's virtue, once lost is hard to regain. The measures to rectify an established pattern of abdication need to be much more severe than those required to stop the first steps in the transfer of control from the guard to his prisoner. A guard assigned to a cellblock in which a large portion of power has been shifted in the past from the officials to the inmates is faced with the weight of precedent; it requires a good deal of moral courage on his part to withstand the aggressive tactics of prisoners who fiercely defend the patterns of corruption established by custom. And if the guard himself has allowed his control to be subverted, he may find that any attempts to undo his error are checked by a threat from the inmate to send a *snitch-kite*—an anonymous note—to the guard's superior officers explaining his past derelictions in detail. This simple form of blackmail may be quite sufficient to maintain the relationships established by friendship, reciprocity, or encroachment.

It is apparent, then, that the power of the custodians is defective, not simply in the sense that the ruled are rebellious, but also in the sense that the rulers are reluctant. We must attach a new meaning to Lord Acton's aphorism that power tends to corrupt and absolute power corrupts absolutely. The custodians of the New Jersey State Prison, far from being converted into brutal tyrants, are under strong pressure to compromise with their captives, for it is a paradox that they can insure their dominance only by allowing it to be corrupted. Only by tolerating violations of "minor" rules and regulations can the guard secure compliance in the "major" areas of the custodial regime. Ill-equipped to maintain the social distance which in theory separates the world of the officials and the world of the inmates, their suspicions eroded by long familiarity, the custodians are led into a modus vivendi with their captives which bears little resemblance to the stereotypical picture of guards and their prisoners.

V

The fact that the officials of the prison experience serious difficulties in imposing their regime on the society of prisoners is sometimes attributed to inadequacies of the custodial staff's personnel. These inadequacies, it is claimed, are in turn due to the fact that more than 50 percent of the guards are temporary employees who have not passed a Civil Service examination. In 1952, for example, a month and a half before the disturbances which dramatically underlined some of the problems of the officials, the Deputy Commissoner of the Department of Institutions and Agencies made the following points in a report concerning the temporary officer of the New Jersey State Prison's custodial force:

1. Because they are not interested in the prison service as a career, the temporary officers tend to have a high turnover as they are quick to resign to accept more remunerative employment.
2. Because they are inexperienced, they are not able to foresee or forestall disciplinary infractions, the on-coming symptoms of which the more experienced officer would detect and take appropriate preventive measures.
3. Because they are not trained as are the regular officers, they do not have the self-confidence that comes with the physical training and defensive measures which are part of the regular officers' pre-service and in-service training and, therefore, it is not uncommon for them to be somewhat timid and inclined to permit the prisoner to take advantage of them.
4. Because many of them are beyond the age limit or cannot meet the physical requirements for regular appointment as established by Civil Service, they cannot look forward to a permanent career and are therefore less interested in the welfare of the institution than their brother officers.
5. Finally, because of the short period of employment, they do not recognize the individual prisoners who are most likely to incite trouble or commit serious infractions, and they are at a disadvantage in dealing with the large groups which congregate in the cellblocks, the messhall, the auditorium, and the yard.[12]

Now the guard at the New Jersey State Prison receives a salary of $3,240 per year when he is hired and he can reach a maximum of $3,840 per year; and there is little doubt that the low salary scale accounts for much of the prison's high turnover rate. The fact that the job of the guard is often depressing, dangerous, and possesses relatively low prestige

[12] See New Jersey Committee to Examine and Investigate the Prison and Parole Systems of New Jersey, *Report*, November 21, 1952.

adds further difficulties. There is also little doubt that the high turnover rate carries numerous evils in its train, as the comments of the Deputy Commissioner have indicated. Yet even if higher salaries could counterbalance the many dissatisfying features of the guard's job—to a point where the custodial force consisted of men with long service rather than a group of transients—there remains a question of whether or not the problems of administration in the New Jersey State Prison would be eased to a significant extent. This, of course, is heresy from the viewpoint of those who trace the failure of social organizations to the personal failings of the individuals who man the organizational structure. Perhaps, indeed, there is some comfort in the idea that if the budget of the prison were larger, if higher salaries could be paid to entice "better" personnel within the walls, if guards could be persuaded to remain for longer periods, then the many difficulties of the prison bureaucracy would disappear. From this point of view, the problems of the custodial institution are rooted in the niggardliness of the free community and the consequent inadequacies of the institution's personnel rather than flaws in the social system of the prison itself. But to suppose that higher salaries are an answer to the plight of the custodians is to suppose, first, that there are men who by reason of their particular skills and personal characteristics are better qualified to serve as guards if they could be recruited; and second, that experience and training within the institution itself will better prepare the guard for his role, if greater financial rewards could convince him to make a career of his prison employment. Both of these suppositions, however, are open to some doubt. There are few jobs in the free community which are comparable to that of the guard in the maximum security prison and which, presumably, could equip the guard-to-be with the needed skills. If the job requirements of the guard's position are not technical skills but turn on matters of character such as courage, honesty, and so on, there is no assurance that men with these traits will flock to the prison if the salary of the guard is increased. And while higher salaries may decrease the turnover rate—thus making an in-service training program feasible and providing a custodial force with greater experience —it is not certain if such a change can lead to marked improvement. A brief period of schooling can familiarize the new guard with the routines of the institution, but to prepare the guard for the realities of his assigned role with lectures and discussions is quite another matter. And it seems entirely possible that prolonged experience in the prison may enmesh the guard deeper and deeper in patterns of compromise and misplaced trust rather than sharpening his drive toward a rigorous enforcement of institutional regulations.

We are not arguing, of course, that the quality of the personnel in the prison is irrelevant to the successful performance of the bureaucracy's tasks nor are we arguing that it would be impossible to improve the quality of the personnel by increasing salaries. We are arguing, however, that the problems of the custodians far transcend the size of the guard's pay check or the length of his employment and that better personnel is at best a palliative rather than a final cure. It is true, of course, that it is difficult to unravel the characteristics of a social organization from the characteristics of the individuals who are its members; but there seems to be little reason to believe that a different crop of guards in the New Jersey State Prison would exhibit an outstanding increase in efficiency in trying to impose the regime of the custodians on the population of prisoners. *The lack of a sense of duty among those who are held captive, the obvious fallacies of coercion, the pathetic collection of rewards and punishments to induce compliance, the strong pressures toward the corruption of the guard in the form of friendship, reciprocity, and the transfer of duties into the hands of trusted inmates—all are structural defects in the prison's system of power rather than individual inadequacies.*[13]

[13] Those who are familiar with prison systems such as those of the Federal government or the State of California might argue that I have underestimated the possibilities of improvement which can be won with well-trained, well-paid, well-led guards. They might be right, but I think it is important to stress the serious, "built-in" weaknesses of the prison as a social system.

The question of whether these defects are inevitable in the custodial institution—or in any system of total power—must be deferred to a later chapter. For the moment it is enough to point out that in the New Jersey State Prison the custodians are unable or unwilling to prevent their captives from committing numerous violations of the rules which make up the theoretical blueprint for behavior and this failure is not a temporary, personal aberration but a built-in feature of the prison social system. It is only by understanding this fact that we can understand the world of the prisoners, since so many significant aspects of inmate behavior—such as coercion of fellow prisoners, fraud, gambling, homosexuality, sharing stolen supplies, and so on—are in clear contravention to institutional regulations. It is the nature of this world which must now claim our attention.

CHAPTER FOUR

THE PAINS OF IMPRISONMENT

IN OUR DISCUSSION of the New Jersey State Prison, the bulk of our remarks has been directed to the custodians—their objectives, their procedures, and their limitations. We have been looking at the prison's system of power from the position of the rulers rather than that of the ruled, and only in passing have we noted the meaning of imprisonment for the prisoners. Now, however, we must examine this society of captives from the viewpoint of the inmates more systematically and in more detail.

It might be argued, of course, that there are certain dangers in speaking of the inmates' perspective of captivity, since it is apt to carry the implication that all prisoners perceive their captivity in precisely the same way. It might be argued that in reality there are as many prisons as there are prisoners—that each man brings to the custodial institution his own needs and his own background and each man takes away from the prison his own interpretation of life within the walls. We do not intend to deny that different men see the conditions of custody somewhat differently and accord these conditions a different emphasis in their personal accounting. Yet when we examine the way the inmates of the New Jersey State Prison perceive the social environment created by the custodians, the dominant fact is the hard core of consensus expressed by the members of the captive population with regard to the nature of their confinement. The inmates are agreed that life in the maximum security prison is depriving or frustrating in the extreme.

In part, the deprivations or frustrations of prison life today might be viewed as punishments which the free community deliberately inflicts on the offender for violating the law; in part, they might be seen as the unplanned (or, as some would argue, the unavoidable) concomitants of confining large groups of criminals for prolonged periods. In either case, the modern pains of imprisonment are often defined by society as a humane alternative to the physical brutality and the neglect which constituted the major meaning of imprisonment in the past. But in examining the pains of imprisonment as they exist today, it is imperative that we go beyond the fact that severe bodily suffering has long since disappeared as a significant aspect of the custodians' regime, leaving behind a residue of apparently less acute hurts such as the loss of liberty, the deprivation of goods and services, the frustration of sexual desire, and so on. These deprivations or frustrations of the modern prison may indeed be the acceptable or unavoidable implications of imprisonment, but we must recognize the fact that they can be just as painful as the physical maltreatment which they have replaced. As Maslow has indicated, there are some frustrating situations which appear as a serious attack on the personality, as a "threat to the life goals of the individual, to his defensive system, to his self-esteem, or to his feelings of security."[1] Such attacks on the psychological level are less easily seen than a sadistic beating, a pair of shackles in the floor, or the caged man on a treadmill, but the destruction of the psyche is no less fearful than bodily affliction and it must play a large role in our discussion. Whatever may be the pains of imprisonment, then, in the custodial institution of today, we must explore the way in which the deprivations and frustrations pose profound threats to the inmate's personality or sense of personal worth.

[1] Cf. A. H. Maslow, "Deprivation, Threat, and Frustration," in *Readings in Social Psychology*, edited by T. M. Newcomb and E. L. Hartley, New York: Henry Holt and Company, 1947.

II

The Deprivation of Liberty

Of all the painful conditions imposed on the inmates of the New Jersey State Prison, none is more immediately obvious than the loss of liberty. The prisoner must live in a world shrunk to thirteen and a half acres and within this restricted area his freedom of movement is further confined by a strict system of passes, the military formations in moving from one point within the institution to another, and the demand that he remain in his cell until given permission to do otherwise. In short, the prisoner's loss of liberty is a double one—first, by confinement to the institution and second, by confinement within the institution.

The mere fact that the individual's movements are restricted, however, is far less serious than the fact that imprisonment means that the inmate is cut off from family, relatives, and friends, not in the self-isolation of the hermit or the misanthrope, but in the involuntary seclusion of the outlaw. It is true that visiting and mailing privileges partially relieve the prisoner's isolation—if he can find someone to visit him or write to him and who will be approved as a visitor or correspondent by the prison officials. Many inmates, however, have found their links with persons in the free community weakening as the months and years pass by. This may explain in part the fact that an examination of the visiting records of a random sample of the inmate population, covering approximately a one-year period, indicated that 41 percent of the prisoners in the New Jersey State Prison had received no visits from the outside world.

It is not difficult to see this isolation as painfully depriving or frustrating in terms of lost emotional relationships, of loneliness and boredom. But what makes this pain of imprisonment bite most deeply is the fact that the confinement of the criminal represents a deliberate, moral rejection of the criminal by the free community. Indeed, as Reckless has pointed out, it is the moral condemnation of the criminal—however

65

it may be symbolized—that converts hurt into punishment, i.e. the just consequence of committing an offense, and it is this condemnation that confronts the inmate by the fact of his seclusion.

Now it is sometimes claimed that many criminals are so alienated from conforming society and so identified with a criminal subculture that the moral condemnation, rejection, or disapproval of legitimate society does not touch them; they are, it is said, indifferent to the penal sanctions of the free community, at least as far as the moral stigma of being defined as a criminal is concerned. Possibly this is true for a small number of offenders such as the professional thief described by Sutherland[2] or the psychopathic personality delineated by William and Joan McCord.[3] For the great majority of criminals in prison, however, the evidence suggests that neither alienation from the ranks of the law-abiding nor involvement in a system of criminal value is sufficient to eliminate the threat to the prisoner's ego posed by society's rejection.[4] The signs pointing to the prisoner's degradation are many—the anonymity of a uniform and a number rather than a name, the shaven head,[5] the insistence on gestures of respect and subordination when addressing officials, and so on. The prisoner is never allowed to forget that, by committing a crime, he has foregone his claim to the status of a full-fledged, *trusted* member of society. The status lost by the prisoner is, in fact, similar to what Marshall has called the status of citizenship—that basic acceptance of the individual as a func-

---

2 Cf. Edwin H. Sutherland, *The Professional Thief*, Chicago: The University of Chicago Press, 1937.

3 Cf. William and Joan McCord, *Psychopathy and Delinquency*, New York: Grune and Stratton, 1956.

4 For an excellent discussion of the symbolic overtones of imprisonment, see Walter C. Reckless, *The Crime Problem*, New York: Appleton-Century-Crofts, Inc., 1955, pp. 428-429.

5 Western culture has long placed a peculiar emphasis on shaving the head as a symbol of degradation, ranging from the enraged treatment of collaborators in occupied Europe to the more measured barbering of recruits in the Armed Forces. In the latter case, as in the prison, the nominal purpose has been cleanliness and neatness, but for the person who is shaved the meaning is somewhat different. In the New Jersey State Prison, the prisoner is clipped to the skull on arrival but not thereafter.

tioning member of the society in which he lives.[6] It is true that in the past the imprisoned criminal literally suffered civil death and that although the doctrines of attainder and corruption of blood were largely abandoned in the 18th and 19th Centuries, the inmate is still stripped of many of his civil rights such as the right to vote, to hold office, to sue in court, and so on.[7] But as important as the loss of these civil rights may be, the loss of that more diffuse status which defines the individual as someone to be trusted or as morally acceptable is the loss which hurts most.

In short, the wall which seals off the criminal, the contaminated man, is a constant threat to the prisoner's self-conception and the threat is continually repeated in the many daily reminders that he must be kept apart from "decent" men. Somehow this rejection or degradation by the free community must be warded off, turned aside, rendered harmless. Somehow the imprisoned criminal must find a device for rejecting his rejectors, if he is to endure psychologically.[8]

The Deprivation of Goods and Services

There are admittedly many problems in attempting to compare the standard of living existing in the free community and the standard of living which is supposed to be the lot of the inmate in prison. How, for example, do we interpret the fact that a covering for the floor of a cell usually consists of a scrap from a discarded blanket and that even this possession is forbidden by the prison authorities? What meaning do we attach to the fact that no inmate owns a common piece of furniture, such as a chair, but only a homemade stool? What is the value of a suit of clothing which is also a convict's uniform with a stripe and a stencilled number? The answers are far from simple although there are a number of prison officials

[6] See T. H. Marshall, *Citizenship and Social Class*, Cambridge, England: The Cambridge University Press, 1950.

[7] Paul W. Tappan, "The Legal Rights of Prisoners," *The Annals of the American Academy of Political and Social Science*, Vol. 293, May 1954, pp. 99-111.

[8] See Lloyd W. McCorkle and Richard R. Korn, "Resocialization Within Walls." *Ibid.*, pp. 88-98.

who will argue that some inmates are better off in prison, in strictly material terms, than they could ever hope to be in the rough-and-tumble economic life of the free community. Possibly this is so, but at least it has never been claimed by the inmates that the goods and services provided the prisoner are equal to or better than the goods and services which the prisoner could obtain if he were left to his own devices outside the walls. The average inmate finds himself in a harshly Spartan environment which he defines as painfully depriving.

Now it is true that the prisoner's basic material needs are met—in the sense that he does not go hungry, cold, or wet. He receives adequate medical care and he has the opportunity for exercise. But a standard of living constructed in terms of so many calories per day, so many hours of recreation, so many cubic yards of space per individual, and so on, misses the central point when we are discussing the individual's feeling of deprivation, however useful it may be in setting minimum levels of consumption for the maintenance of health. A standard of living can be hopelessly inadequate, from the individual's viewpoint, because it bores him to death or fails to provide those subtle symbolic overtones which we invest in the world of possessions. And this is the core of the prisoner's problem in the area of goods and services. He wants—or needs, if you will—not just the so-called necessities of life but also the amenities: cigarettes and liquor as well as calories, interesting foods as well as sheer bulk, individual clothing as well as adequate clothing, individual furnishings for his living quarters as well as shelter, privacy as well as space. The "rightfulness" of the prisoner's feeling of deprivation can be questioned. And the objective reality of the prisoner's deprivation—in the sense that he has actually suffered a fall from his economic position in the free community—can be viewed with skepticism, as we have indicated above. But these criticisms are irrelevant to the significant issue, namely that legitimately or illegitimately, rationally or irrationally, the inmate population defines its present material impoverishment as a painful loss.

Now in modern Western culture, material possessions are so large a part of the individual's conception of himself that to be stripped of them is to be attacked at the deepest layers of personality. This is particularly true when poverty cannot be excused as a blind stroke of fate or a universal calamity. Poverty due to one's own mistakes or misdeeds represents an indictment against one's basic value or personal worth and there are few men who can philosophically bear the want caused by their own actions. It is true some prisoners in the New Jersey State Prison attempt to interpret their low position in the scale of goods and services as an effort by the State to exploit them economically. Thus, in the eyes of some inmates, the prisoner is poor not because of an offense which he has committed in the past but because the State is a tyrant which uses its captive criminals as slave labor under the hypocritical guise of reformation. Penology, it is said, is a racket. Their poverty, then, is not punishment as we have used the word before, i.e. the just consequence of criminal behavior; rather, it is an unjust hurt or pain inflicted without legitimate cause. This attitude, however, does not appear to be particularly widespread in the inmate population and the great majority of prisoners must face their privation without the aid of the wronged man's sense of injustice. Furthermore, most prisoners are unable to fortify themselves in their low level of material existence by seeing it as a means to some high or worthy end. They are unable to attach any significant meaning to their need to make it more bearable, such as present pleasures foregone for pleasures in the future, self-sacrifice in the interests of the community, or material asceticism for the purpose of spiritual salvation.

The inmate, then, sees himself as having been made poor by reason of his own acts and without the rationale of compensating benefits. The failure is *his* failure in a world where control and possession of the material environment are commonly taken as sure indicators of a man's worth. It is true that our society, as materialistic as it may be, does not rely exclusively on goods and services as a criterion of an individual's value; and, as we shall see shortly, the inmate population defends itself by stressing alternative or supplementary measures of merit. But impoverishment remains as one of the most bitter attacks on the individual's self-image that our society has to offer and the prisoner cannot ignore the implications of his straitened cirumstances.[9] Whatever the discomforts and irritations of the prisoner's Spartan existence may be, he must carry the additional burden of social definitions which equate his material deprivation with personal inadequacy.

The Deprivation of Heterosexual Relationships

Unlike the prisoner in many Latin-American countries, the inmate of the maximum security prison in New Jersey does not enjoy the privilege of so-called conjugal visits. And in those brief times when the prisoner is allowed to see his wife, mistress, or "female friend," the woman must sit on one side of a plate glass window and the prisoner on the other, communicating by means of a phone under the scrutiny of a guard. If the inmate, then, is rejected and impoverished by the facts of his imprisonment, he is also figuratively castrated by his involuntary celibacy.

Now a number of writers have suggested that men in prison undergo a reduction of the sexual drive and that the sexual frustrations of prisoners are therefore less than they might appear to be at first glance. The reports of reduced sexual interest have, however, been largely confined to accounts of men imprisoned in concentration camps or similar extreme situations where starvation, torture, and physical exhaustion have reduced life to a simple struggle for survival or left the captive sunk in apathy. But in the American prison these

---

[9] Komarovsky's discussion of the psychological implications of unemployment is particularly apposite here, despite the markedly different context, for she notes that economic failure provokes acute anxiety as humiliation cuts away at the individual's conception of his manhood. He feels useless, undeserving of respect, disorganized, adrift in a society where economic status is a major anchoring point. Cf. Mirra Komarovsky, *The Unemployed Man and His Family*, New York: The Dryden Press, 1940, pp. 74-77.

factors are not at work to any significant extent and Linder has noted that the prisoner's access to mass media, pornography circulated among inmates, and similar stimuli serve to keep alive the prisoner's sexual impulses.[10] The same thought is expressed more crudely by the inmates of the New Jersey State Prison in a variety of obscene expressions and it is clear that the lack of heterosexual intercourse is a frustrating experience for the imprisoned criminal and that it is a frustration which weighs heavily and painfully on his mind during his prolonged confinement. There are, or course, some "habitual" homosexuals in the prison—men who were homosexuals before their arrival and who continue their particular form of deviant behavior within the all-male society of the custodial institution. For these inmates, perhaps, the deprivation of heterosexual intercourse cannot be counted as one of the pains of imprisonment. They are few in number, however, and are only too apt to be victimized or raped by aggressive prisoners who have turned to homosexuality as a temporary means of relieving their frustration.

Yet as important as frustration in the sexual sphere may be in physiological terms, the psychological problems created by the lack of heterosexual relationships can be even more serious. A society composed exclusively of men tends to generate anxieties in its members concerning their masculinity regardless of whether or not they are coerced, bribed, or seduced into an overt homosexual liaison. Latent homosexual tendencies may be activated in the individual without being translated into open behavior and yet still arouse strong guilt feelings at either the conscious or unconscious level. In the tense atmosphere of the prison with its known perversions, its importunities of admitted homosexuals, and its constant references to the problems of sexual frustration by guards and inmates alike, there are few prisoners who can escape the fact that an essential component of a man's self conception—his status of male—is called into question. And if an

10 See Robert M. Lindner, "Sex in Prison," *Complex*, Vol. 6, Fall 1951, pp. 5-20.

inmate has in fact engaged in homosexual behavior within the walls, not as a continuation of an habitual pattern but as a rare act of sexual deviance under the intolerable pressure of mounting physical desire, the psychological onslaughts on his ego image will be particularly acute.[11]

In addition to these problems stemming from sexual frustration per se, the deprivation of heterosexual relationships carries with it another threat to the prisoner's image of himself—more diffuse, perhaps, and more difficult to state precisely and yet no less disturbing. The inmate is shut off from the world of women which by its very polarity gives the male world much of its meaning. Like most men, the inmate must search for his identity not simply within himself but also in the picture of himself which he finds reflected in the eyes of others; and since a significant half of his audience is denied him, the inmate's self image is in danger of becoming half complete, fractured, a monochrome without the hues of reality. The prisoner's looking-glass self, in short—to use Cooley's fine phrase—is only that portion of the prisoner's personality which is recognized or appreciated by men and this partial identity is made hazy by the lack of contrast.

[11] Estimates of the proportion of inmates who engage in homosexuality during their confinement in the prison are apt to vary. In the New Jersey State Prison, however, Wing Guards and Shop Guards examined a random sample of inmates who were well known to them from prolonged observation and identified 35 percent of the men as individuals believed to have engaged in homosexual acts. The judgments of these officials were substantially in agreement with the judgments of a prisoner who possessed an apparently well-founded reputation as an aggressive homosexual deeply involved in patterns of sexual deviance within the institution and who had been convicted of sodomy. But the validity of these judgments remains largely unknown and we present the following conclusions, based on a variety of sources, as provisional at best: First, a fairly large proportion of prisoners engage in homosexual behavior during their period of confinement. Second, for many of those prisoners who do engage in homosexual behavior, their sexual deviance is rare or sporadic rather than chronic. And third, as we have indicated before, much of the homosexuality which does occur in prison is not part of a life pattern existing before and after confinement; rather, it is a response to the peculiar rigors of imprisonment. A further discussion of the meaning and range of sexual behavior in the New Jersey State Prison will be presented in the next chapter.

The Deprivation of Autonomy

We have noted before that the inmate suffers from what we have called a loss of autonomy in that he is subjected to a vast body of rules and commands which are designed to control his behavior in minute detail. To the casual observer, however, it might seem that the many areas of life in which self-determination is withheld, such as the language used in a letter, the hours of sleeping and eating, or the route to work, are relatively unimportant. Perhaps it might be argued, as in the case of material deprivation, that the inmate in prison is not much worse off than the individual in the free community who is regulated in a great many aspects of his life by the iron fist of custom. It could even be argued, as some writers have done, that for a number of imprisoned criminals the extensive control of the custodians provides a welcome escape from freedom and that the prison officials thus supply an external Super-Ego which serves to reduce the anxieties arising from an awareness of deviant impulses. But from the viewpoint of the inmate population, it is precisely the triviality of much of the officials' control which often proves to be most galling. Regulation by a bureaucratic staff is felt far differently than regulation by custom. And even though a few prisoners do welcome the strict regime of the custodians as a means of checking their own aberrant behavior which they would like to curb but cannot, most prisoners look on the matter in a different light. Most prisoners, in fact, express an intense hostility against their far-reaching dependence on the decisions of their captors and the restricted ability to make choices must be included among the pains of imprisonment along with restrictions of physical liberty, the possession of goods and services, and heterosexual relationships.

Now the loss of autonomy experienced by the inmates of the prison does not represent a grant of power freely given by the ruled to the rulers for a limited and specific end. Rather, it is total and it is imposed—and for these reasons it is less endurable. The nominal objectives of the custodians are not,

73

in general, the objectives of the prisoners.[12] Yet regardless of whether or not the inmate population shares some aims with the custodial bureaucracy, the many regulations and orders of the New Jersey State Prison's official regime often arouse the prisoner's hostility because they don't "make sense" from the prisoner's point of view. Indeed, the incomprehensible order or rule is a basic feature of life in prison. Inmates, for example, are forbidden to take food from the messhall to their cells. Some prisoners see this as a move designed to promote cleanliness; others are convinced that the regulation is for the purpose of preventing inmates from obtaining anything that might be used in the *sub rosa* system of barter. Most, however, simply see the measure as another irritating, pointless gesture of authoritarianism. Similarly, prisoners are denied parole but are left in ignorance of the reasons for the decision. Prisoners are informed that the delivery of mail will be delayed—but they are not told why.

Now some of the inmate population's ignorance might be described as "accidental"; it arises from what we can call the principle of bureaucratic indifference, i.e., events which seem important or vital to those at the bottom of the heap are viewed with an increasing lack of concern with each step upward. The rules, the commands, the decisions which flow down to those who are controlled are not accompanied by explanations on the grounds that it is "impractical" or "too much trouble." Some of the inmate population's ignorance, however, is deliberately fostered by the prison officials in that

---

12 We have suggested earlier, in our discussion of the defects of prison as a system of power, that the nominal objectives of the officials tend to be compromised as they are translated into the actual routines of day-to-day life. The modus vivendi reached by guards and their prisoners is oriented toward certain goals which are in fact shared by captors and captives. In this limited sense, the control of the prison officials is partly concurred in by the inmates as well as imposed on them from above. We will explore this issue at greater length in the analysis of crisis and equilibrium in the society of captives, but in discussing the pains of imprisonment our attention is focused on the frustrations or threats posed by confinement rather than the devices which meet these frustrations or threats and render them tolerable. Our interest here is in the vectors of the prison's social system—if we may use an analogy from the physical sciences—rather than the resultant.

explanations are often withheld as a matter of calculated policy. Providing explanations carries an implication that those who are ruled have a right to know—and this in turn suggests that if the explanations are not satisfactory, the rule or order will be changed. But this is in direct contradiction to the theoretical power relationship of the inmates and the prison officials. Imprisoned criminals are individuals who are being punished by society and they must be brought to their knees. If the inmate population maintains the right to argue with its captors, it takes on the appearance of an enemy nation with its own sovereignty; and in so doing it raises disturbing questions about the nature of the offender's deviance. The criminal is no longer simply a man who has broken the law; he has become a part of a group with an alternative viewpoint and thus attacks the validity of the law itself. The custodians' refusal to give reasons for many aspects of their regime can be seen in part as an attempt to avoid such an intolerable situation.

The indignation aroused by the "bargaining inmate" or the necessity of justifying the custodial regime is particularly evident during a riot when prisoners have the "impudence" to present a list of demands. In discussing the disturbances at the New Jersey State Prison in the Spring of 1952, for example, a newspaper editorial angrily noted that "the storm, like a nightmarish April Fool's dream, has passed, leaving in its wake a partially wrecked State Prison as a debasing monument to the ignominious rage of desperate men."

The important point, however, is that the frustration of the prisoner's ability to make choices and the frequent refusals to provide an explanation for the regulations and commands descending from the bureaucratic staff involve a profound threat to the prisoner's self image because they reduce the prisoner to the weak, helpless, dependent status of childhood. As Bettelheim has tellingly noted in his comments on the concentration camp, men under guard stand in constant danger of losing their identification with the normal definition of an adult and the imprisoned criminal finds his picture of himself as a self-determining individual being destroyed by the regime of the custodians.[13] It is possible that this psychological attack is particularly painful in American culture because of the deep-lying insecurities produced by the delays, the conditionality and the uneven progress so often observed in the granting of adulthood. It is also possible that the criminal is frequently an individual who has experienced great difficulty in adjusting himself to figures of authority and who finds the many restraints of prison life particularly threatening in so far as earlier struggles over the establishment of self are reactivated in a more virulent form. But without asserting that Americans in general or criminals in particular are notably ill-equipped to deal with the problems posed by the deprivation of autonomy, the helpless or dependent status of the prisoner clearly represents a serious threat to the prisoner's self image as a fully accredited member of adult society. And of the many threats which may confront the individual, either in or out of prison, there are few better calculated to arouse acute anxieties than the attempt to reimpose the subservience of youth. Public humiliation, enforced respect and deference, the finality of authoritarian decisions, the demands for a specified course of conduct because, in the judgment of another, it is in the individual's best interest— all are features of childhood's helplessness in the face of a superior adult world. Such things may be both irksome and disturbing for a child, especially if the child envisions himself as having outgrown such servitude. But for the adult who has escaped such helplessness with the passage of years, to be thrust back into childhood's helplessness is even more painful, and the inmate of the prison must somehow find a means of coping with the issue.

The Deprivation of Security

However strange it may appear that society has chosen to reduce the criminality of the offender by forcing him to as-

---

[13] Cf. Bruno Bettelheim, "Individual and Mass Behavior in Extreme Situations," in *Readings in Social Psychology*, edited by T. M. Newcomb and E. L. Hartley, New York: Henry Holt and Company, 1947.

sociate with more than a thousand other criminals for years on end, there is one meaning of this involuntary union which is obvious—the individual prisoner is thrown into prolonged intimacy with other men who in many cases have a long history of violent, aggressive behavior. It is a situation which can prove to be anxiety-provoking even for the hardened recidivist and it is in this light that we can understand the comment of an inmate of the New Jersey State Prison who said, "The worst thing about prison is you have to live with other prisoners."

The fact that the imprisoned criminal sometimes views his fellow prisoners as "vicious" or "dangerous" may seem a trifle unreasonable. Other inmates, after all, are men like himself, bearing the legal stigma of conviction. But even if the individual prisoner believes that he himself is not the sort of person who is likely to attack or exploit weaker and less resourceful fellow captives, he is apt to view others with more suspicion. And if he himself is prepared to commit crimes while in prison, he is likely to feel that many others will be at least equally ready. In the next chapter, we will examine the solidarity and the exploitation which actually exist among prisoners, but for the moment it is enough to point out that regardless of the patterns of mutual aid and support which may flourish in the inmate population, there are a sufficient number of outlaws within this group of outlaws to deprive the average prisoner of that sense of security which comes from living among men who can be reasonably expected to abide by the rules of society. While it is true that every prisoner does not live in the constant fear of being robbed or beaten, the constant companionship of thieves, rapists, murderers, and aggressive homosexuals is far from reassuring.

An important aspect of this disturbingly problematical world is the fact that the inmate is acutely aware that sooner or later he will be "tested"—that someone will "push" him to see how far they can go and that he must be prepared to fight for the safety of his person and his possessions. If he should fail, he will thereafter be an object of contempt, constantly in danger of being attacked by other inmates who view him as an obvious victim, as a man who cannot or will not defend his rights. And yet if he succeeds, he may well become a target for the prisoner who wishes to prove himself, who seeks to enhance his own prestige by defeating the man with a reputation for toughness. Thus both success and failure in defending one's self against the aggressions of fellow captives may serve to provoke fresh attacks and no man stands assured of the future.[14]

The prisoner's loss of security arouses acute anxiety, in short, not just because violent acts of aggression and exploitation occur but also because such behavior constantly calls into question the individual's ability to cope with it, in terms of his own inner resources, his courage, his "nerve." Can he stand up and take it? Will he prove to be tough enough? These uncertainties constitute an ego threat for the individual forced to live in prolonged intimacy with criminals, regardless of the nature or extent of his own criminality; and we can catch a glimpse of this tense and fearful existence in the comment of one prisoner who said, "It takes a pretty good man to be able to stand on an equal plane with a guy that's in for rape, with a guy that's in for murder, with a man who's well respected in the institution because he's a real tough cookie. . . ." His expectations concerning the conforming behavior of others destroyed, unable and unwilling to rely on the officials for protection, uncertain of whether or not today's joke will be tomorrow's bitter insult, the prison inmate can never feel safe. And at a deeper level lies the anxiety about his reactions to this unstable world, for then his manhood will be evaluated in the public view.

III

Imprisonment, then, is painful. The pains of imprisonment, however, cannot be viewed as being limited to the loss

---

[14] As the Warden of the New Jersey State Prison has pointed out, the arrival of an obviously tough professional hoodlum creates a serious problem for the recognized "bad man" in a cellblock who is expected to challenge the newcomer immediately.

of physical liberty. The significant hurts lie in the frustrations or deprivations which attend the withdrawal of freedom, such as the lack of heterosexual relationships, isolation from the free community, the withholding of goods and services, and so on. And however painful these frustrations or deprivations may be in the immediate terms of thwarted goals, discomfort, boredom, and loneliness, they carry a more profound hurt as a set of threats or attacks which are directed against the very foundations of the prisoner's being. The individual's picture of himself as a person of value—as a morally acceptable, adult male who can present some claim to merit in his material achievements and his inner strength—begins to waver and grow dim. Society did not plan this onslaught, it is true, and society may even "point with pride" to its humanity in the modern treatment of the criminal. But the pains of imprisonment remain and it is imperative that we recognize them, for they provide the energy for the society of captives as a system of action.

Before we examine how the inmate population actually sets about its task of relieving the pains of imprisonment, however, it is worth while to look at other reactions to the bitter frustrations and threats of confinement which do *not* occur or occur but seldom. By so doing we can better understand the strength of those reactions which do take place. The pains of imprisonment generate enormous pressure which is translated into behavior with all the greater vigor because, like a body of steam under heavy compression with only a few outlets, the body of prisoners is limited in modes of adaptation.[15]

Now if men are confronted with a painfully frustrating situation, they can of course attempt to solve their problem by literally escaping from the situation by means of physical withdrawal. In the case of the inmates of the maximum security prison, however, it is hardly necessary to point out that such

[15] Robert K. Merton's discussion of types of reaction to frustrating situations, i.e. conformity, innovation, ritualism, retreatism, and rebellion, provides an excellent starting point for our analysis. His typology, however, has been changed to meet the specific details of our study. Cf. Robert K. Merton, "Social Structure and Anomie," in *Social Theory and Social Structure*, Glencoe, Ill.: The Free Press, 1949.

a solution is diametrically opposed on the premise on which their world is founded. Perhaps for a few prisoners (the so-called *escape artists*, for example), dreams of flight, however impractical, mercifully disguise the harsh meaning of imprisonment. Their lives are plans for the future rather than present realities.[16] But for most of the inmates, the most obvious solution to the pains of imprisonment is ruled out, as we have indicated in an earlier chapter, and the prisoner must solve his problems within the closely-guarded frontier that is the Wall, if he is to solve his problems at all.

Yet there is another kind of escape from the prison which is at least theoretically possible, i.e. psychological withdrawal. This can take the form of renouncing the goals, the drives, or the needs which are frustrated, either consciously or unconsciously, leaving the prisoner immune in apathy or seeking the gratifications of sublimation. Or it can take the form of a withdrawal into fantasy based on fondled memories of the past or imaginary dramas of life after release. There are a number of inmates in the New Jersey State Prison who have so managed to escape the rigors of their existence, but it is not the path of the majority of prisoners. Perhaps the goals which are frustrated are too important, too vital, to be relinquished by the majority of men. Perhaps the tendency toward a full-fledged retreat into a world of fantasy is reserved for the few who were but lightly linked with reality before their confinement. In any case, most inmates fail to escape the pains of imprisonment by means of these psychological mechanisms just as surely as they fail to escape by physically forcing a breach in the wall and the attacks on the self must be countered in other terms.

If men in prison cannot cure their ills by these modes of retreat, there still remains the possibility of rebellion or innovation. The inmates could try to overthrow or change the custodial regime to ease the frustrations and deprivations which

16 The accounts of soldiers captured during the last war vividly illustrate how planning to escape was used, sometimes quite deliberately, to divert the captive's attention from his existing plight. See also Alban M. Philip, *The Prison-Breakers*, New York: Henry Holt and Company (no year given).

plague them. It is true, of course, that in the event of an open battle, victory inevitably lies in the hands of the guards. Yet men will revolt in a desperate situation even though they know there is no chance of success; the certainty of failure is only one of the reasons why prisoners do not band together in open conflict against their rulers.[17] Of equal or greater importance is the fact that the inmate population is shot through with a variety of ethnic and social cleavages which sharply reduce the possibility of continued mass action called for by an uprising. The inmates lack an ideological commitment transcending their individual differences and the few riots which do occur are as likely to collapse from dissension among prisoners as from repression by the custodial force. One notable exception to this point is to be found in the passive resistance movements of conscientious objectors confined in Federal Prisons during World War II; but the inmates of the New Jersey State Prison have never achieved this degree of organization.

If forceful change is avoided as a solution to the pains of imprisonment in the ordinary course of events, attempts at peaceful change through the use of persuasion are no less rare. The prisoners are well aware that the custodians face a public which would not permit the removal of confinement's frustrations even if they—the custodians—desired to do so. Perhaps it would be more accurate to say that the public *might* allow conjugal visits, furloughs in the free community, a higher standard of living, and so on. But if such changes will come, they will probably come in the somewhat distant future and the persuasive arguments of imprisoned criminals will be a minor factor in bringing these innovations about. The inmate population has little hope of solving problems here and now by the gentle tactics of orderly political activity. Efforts at change from below remain in the form of an individual letter

---

[17] A revolt—a riot—may fail, of course, in the sense that prisoners do not permanently seize the reins of power, yet it may succeed by arousing public opinion so that the conditions of imprisonment are eased. Public outcries for "reforms," however, quickly die away when the *status quo* is re-established.

to the governor, an isolated complaint to the newspapers, or an occasional petition presented to the Warden.

Unable to escape either physically or psychologically, lacking the cohesion to carry through an insurrection that is bound to fail in any case, and bereft of faith in peaceful innovation, the inmate population might seem to have no recourse but the simple endurance of the pains of imprisonment. The frustrations and deprivations of confinement, with their attendant attacks on the prisoner's self image, would strike the prisoner with full force and the time spent in prison would have to be marked down as time spent in purgatory. And to a large extent this is what does happen in reality. There are no exits for the inmate in the sense of a device or series of devices which can completely eliminate the pains of imprisonment. *But if the rigors of confinement cannot be completely removed, they can at least be mitigated by the patterns of social interaction established among the inmates themselves.* In this apparently simple fact lies the key to our understanding of the prisoner's world.

Frustrated not as an individual but as one of many, the inmate finds two paths open. On the one hand, he can attempt to bind himself to his fellow captives with ties of mutal aid, loyalty, affection, and respect, firmly standing in opposition to the officials. On the other hand, he can enter into a war of all against all in which he seeks his own advantage without reference to the claims or needs of other prisoners. In the former case, the rigors of the environment are met with group cohesion or inmate solidarity. Toleration replaces "touchiness," fellow prisoners are persons to be helped rather than exploited, and group allegiance emerges as a dominant value. The inmate's orientation is "collectivistic."[18] In the latter case, the rigors of the environment elicit an alienated response. Abhorrence or indifference feed the frictions of prison life. Fellow prisoners are persons to be exploited by every expedient that comes to hand; the officials are simply another hazard in the

---

[18] Cf. Talcott Parsons and Edward A. Shils (eds.), *Toward a General Theory of Action*, Cambridge, Mass.: Harvard University Press, 1951.

pursuit of the inmate's goals and he stands ready to betray his fellow captives if it advances his interests. The inmate's orientation can be termed "individualistic."[19]

In actuality, the patterns of social interaction among inmates are to be found scattered between these two theoretical extremes. The population of prisoners does not exhibit a perfect solidarity yet neither is the population of prisoners a warring aggregate. Rather, it is a mixture of both and the society of captives lies balanced in an uneasy compromise. It is the nature of this imperfect solution to the pains of imprisonment, seen as a system of social roles, which we will examine in the following chapter.

[19] *Ibid.*

CHAPTER FIVE

ARGOT ROLES

"THE DEVELOPMENT of special languages for special groups organized within the framework of the larger society," says M. M. Lewis in his book *Language and Society*, "is a phenomenon common in the social history of language."[1] The argot of the inmates in the maximum security prison illustrates his point well. Pungent, vivid, racy, and irreverent, the parlance of prisoners "reflects the personality of the inmates who employ it, as well as the conflicts and tensions inherent in the institutional setting. It is the language of the dispossessed, tinged with bitterness and marked by a self-lacerating humor."[2]

A portion of this argot is evidently drawn from the language of the underworld and the current slang of the United States. In addition, one can detect traces of an international criminal language which, according to Mencken, was transported to America in the early part of the 19th Century when many professional thieves were driven out of London by Sir Robert Peel's metropolitan police.[3] And we can find a number of words borrowed from the jargon of prostitutes, tramps, beggars, carnival workers, and jazz addicts. But whatever may be the roots of prison argot, its importance for our present analysis lies in the fact that it provides a map of the inmate social system.

[1] M. M. Lewis, *Language in Society*, New York: Social Science Publishers, 1948, p. 45.
[2] David Boroff, "A Study of Reformatory Argot," *American Speech*, Vol. XXVI, No. 3, October 1951, p. 190.
[3] H. L. Mencken, *The American Language*, New York: Alfred A. Knopf, 1937, pp. 575-589.

84

Now some writers have claimed that the argot of criminals functions to maintain secrecy; it is a device for keeping the law-abiding in ignorance. I find this theory somewhat doubtful, however, and it is particularly questionable in the prison where the guards know the meaning of argot terms as well as the prisoners. A professional thief, for example, has pointed out that the criminal immediately discloses his intentions to the forces of law and order if he uses criminal argot in public.[4] A number of writers, noting this identifying function of criminal argot, have argued that the language of the underworld, far from being used as a means of secrecy, is of greatest importance as a distinguishing symbol. The argot of criminals serves as an expression of group loyalty and group membership. And the imprisoned offender, it is held, indicates his allegiance to the inmate population by using its special vocabulary. Yet I think this too is somewhat doubtful, since there are many prison officials who not only know the meaning of the inmates' argot but also use it constantly in their daily speech. It is true that we might take this as a partial indication of the guard's corruption mentioned previously, and it is true that guards sometimes feel that sharing a special language with the inmates has brought them too close to the inmate world—just as the excessive use of undergraduate slang by a member of a university faculty creates some uneasiness. And it is true that inmates feel that a person who speaks in terms of their lexicon is something other than a stranger, although he may remain hard to define. But this view of argot's use as an indicator of loyalty or allegiance seems to be secondary and both guards and inmates are aware that a language can be used without necessarily signifying commitment to a group's values. Instead, the more critical function of prison argot would appear to be its utility in ordering and classifying experience within the walls in terms which deal specifically with the major problems of prison life.

As Strong has pointed out, social groups are apt to characterize individuals in terms of crucial "axes of life," or lines

---

[4] Edwin H. Sutherland, *The Professional Thief*, Chicago: The University of Chicago Press, 1937.

of interests, problems, and concerns which the group faces, and then attach distinctive names to the resulting types or typical social roles.[5] By so doing, the group provides itself with a sort of shorthand which compresses the variegated range of its experience into a manageable framework. By distinguishing and naming we prepare ourselves for action—and, indeed, as Malinowski has suggested, a good part of action itself is a matter of distinguishing and naming.[6] The activities of group members are no longer an undifferentiated stream of events; rather, they have been analyzed, classified, given labels; and these labels supply an evaluation and interpretation of experience as well as a set of convenient names. Words in the prison argot, no less than words in ordinary usage, carry a penumbra of admiration and disapproval, of attitude and belief, which channels and controls the behavior of the individual who uses them or to whom they are applied.

As group experiences come to differ more and more from those of the larger community of which the group is a part—as new patterns of behavior arise demanding evaluation and interpretation—the language of the group begins to change. Behavior which is not distinguished by the larger community takes on a different importance and receives a special label. New words are invented or old words are applied in a new and often more restricted way; the skein of reality is being cut in an unfamiliar fashion. In short, different experiences mean a different language and the result—in the prison, at least—is argot. The society of captives exhibits a number of distinctive tags for the distinctive social roles played by its members in response to the particular problems of imprisonment. It is these patterns of behavior, recognized and labelled by the inmates of the New Jersey State Prison, which we have chosen to call argot roles and which now occupy our attention.

[5] See S. A. Strong, "Social Types in a Minority Group," *The American Journal of Sociology*, Vol. 48, March 1943, pp. 563-573.
[6] See Bronislaw Malinowski, *Magic, Science, and Religion*, Garden City, New York: Doubleday & Company, Inc., 1955, p. 34.

II

Rats and Center Men

The flow of information in any social group is always imperfect, if we define perfect communication as the transmission of all information to all group members with equal speed and without error. Of particular interest, however, is the imperfection which arises from two or more "circuits" in the network of communication. Certain types of information are prohibited from flowing across social boundaries erected within the group and deception, hypocrisy, spying, and betrayal emerge as crucial social events.

The most obvious social boundary in the custodial institution is, of course, that which exists between captors and captives; and inmates argue fiercely that a prisoner should never give any information to the custodians which will act to the detriment of a fellow captive. Since the most trivial piece of information may, all unwittingly, lead to another inmate's downfall, the ban on communication is extended to cover all but the most routine matters. The bureaucracy of custodians and the population of prisoners are supposed to struggle in silence.

The word *rat* or *squealer* is a familiar label for the man who betrays his fellows by violating the ban on communication and it is used in this sense in the prison. But in the prison the word *rat* or *squealer* carries an emotional significance far greater than that usually encountered in the free community. The name is never applied lightly as a joking insult—as is often the case with the numerous obscene expressions which lard the conversation of prisoners. Instead, it represents the most serious accusation that one inmate can level against another, for it implies a betrayal that transcends the specific act of disclosure. The *rat* is a man who has betrayed not just one inmate or several; he has betrayed inmates in general by denying the cohesion of prisoners as a dominant value when confronting the world of officialdom.[7]

[7] Talcott Parsons has commented on the same idea in noting that the deviant's compulsive need for group membership "may have an important

Most of the *ratting* that occurs in the prison is done for the sake of personal gain, but we can distinguish two different forms. First, there are those *rats* who reveal their own identity to the officials, who hope to win preferential treatment from their rulers in exchange for information. The following note, originally block printed in red crayon on a scrap of paper and left in the Center, can serve as an illustration:

IF YOU LIKE YOU CAN GET A BASKET OF STOVES, SWAG COFFEE,[8] AND MANY SURPRISING ITEMS IF YOU TAKE AND PULL A SURPRISE SEARCH EARLY IN THE MORNING BEFORE RUNNERS ARE OUT OR AFTER SUPPER. BEST TIME 6:AM OR RIGHT AFTER GET UP BELL IN 2 LEFT. LOOK IN THE CELLS OF INMATES A———, B———, C———, D———, E———. IN 6 LEFT, LOOK IN THE CELLS OF INMATES H———, I———, K———. COFFEE IS FROM HEAD-WAITER OFFICER DINING ROOM, COOKHOUSE COFFEE MAN IN-MATE DINING ROOM AND ICEBOX MAN. LOOK THESE CELLS OVER AND SEE IF I'M NOT RIGHT. DON'T FLASH THIS OR YOU WON'T CATCH ANYONE. YOU GOT LEAK IN THE CENTER. ON RECEIVING THINGS LIKE THIS SOME LETTERS ARE PICKED UP AND READ BY THE INMATES AND LAID BACK ON THE CENTER DESK AFTER THEY ARE LOOKED OVER FOR A SIGNITURE. WHY DON'T YOU SUPERVISE THIS YOURSELF AND YOU WILL SEE A LOT OF THINGS. A LOT OF OFFICERS JUST GO IN A CELL—IF IT IS A FRIEND THEY JUST WALK OUT. CAN'T FIND ANYTHING IN THAT CELL. OUT IT GOES WITH THE INMATE. THE COPS DON'T LOOK. TOO MUCH WORK. NO COFFEE IN THE STORE YET. BET YOU WILL FIND IN THESE CELLS OVER 20 POUNDS AND ALL COOKHOUSE AS COMPARE THE GRIND. YOU WILL SEE NOT FROM THE STORE BUT FROM COOKHOUSE. I KNOW. I SEE IT GO OUT SO MY BUDDY AND I DECIDED TO TELL YOU. SO DO US A FAVOR. DON'T PASS THIS LETTER ABOUT. THANKS. WE GOT YOU THIS. MORE YET MAYBE.

LOOK IN SUGAR BOXES. ALSO IN TOBACCO CANS FOR POUNDS OF COFFEE, STOVES. SAY GOT ON STORE ORDER. GOOD STORY, NO?

Inmate L———
Inmate M———

---

bearing on various features of . . . delinquent sub-culture groups, such as the extreme concern with loyalty to the group and the violence of the condemnation of 'ratting.' " Cf. Talcott Parsons, *The Social System*, Glencoe, Ill.: The Free Press, 1951, pp. 286-287.

[8] The word *swag* is used in the prison both as an adjective and a noun in referring to contraband.

Second, there are those *rats* who prefer to remain anonymous, not because their betrayal is an unselfish act committed for the good of the custodians, but because they wish to get rid of a competitor or to settle a grudge. Thus the officials may find themselves being manipulated by their prisoners into a position where they are serving unintentionally as a weapon in the battles taking place among the inmates. There is always the danger that they will be gulled in the process, for the anonymous *rat* does not need to fear official retaliation if he supplies false information. The *rat*, in short, may be a liar as well as a betrayer and he threatens the innocent as well as the guilty.

Now to view the *rat* or the *squealer* as a man playing a social role is to view betrayal not as an isolated piece of behavior but as a part of a larger system of action, i.e. the patterns of interaction among guards and inmates. We have suggested that an important aspect of this system is the social boundary separating captors and captives into two "circuits" of communication and that the prisoner who transmits information across the boundary is usually pursuing his own interests at the expense of his fellow prisoners. There is another way of crossing the boundary, however, of being disloyal to the inmate world, which does not involve the disclosure of secrets, which is only partially a matter of personal aggrandizement, and yet which arouses great contempt. An inmate can take on the opinions, attitudes, and beliefs of the custodians. In the New Jersey State Prison, such an inmate is labelled a *center man*, apparently in reference to the Center which serves as the officials' seat of government.[9]

The phenomenon of men identifying themselves with their oppressors—of publicly proclaiming the virtues of the rulers, expressing their values, or, still worse in the eyes of the inmates, obeying them too gladly—may represent a deliberate, Machiavellian attempt to flatter those who have power in order to gain favors. The inmates of the New Jersey State Prison believe, however, that the *center man* is frequently an in-

9 See pages 4-5.

dividual who sides with the officials not because he thinks he can hoodwink his captors but because he actually shares their viewpoint. As one prisoner has said, "The *center man* is a man who's always willing to get along with the institutional officials. He'll bend over backwards to do it. He'll go out of his way. I have one word that seems to fit all of them—servile. They're always bowing and scraping. . . ." It is difficult, of course, to distinguish manipulative fawning from the deference of sincere conviction and the problem is made still more difficult in the prison by the fact that the society of captives is so polarized that anything but unwavering contempt for the guards is defined by the inmates as a sign of abject weakness.[10] But the inmates would seem to be right in believing that disloyalty need not spring from a conscious, deliberate plan to advance one's interests. If the *rat* is a man who pretends to be on the side of the inmates and yet betrays them, the *center man* is a man who makes no secret of where his sympathies lie. His disloyalty is open. And if the *rat* is hated for his deception and his hypocrisy, the *center man* is despised for his slavish submission. But whether a man attempts to escape the rigors of imprisonment by exchanging information for preferential treatment, or, more subtly, by identifying himself with his rulers, he has destroyed the unity of inmates as they face their rejectors. The population of prisoners—the one group to which the inmate can turn for prestige, for approval, for acceptance—has been weakened by his behavior and it is in this light that we must understand his condemnation.

Gorillas and Merchants

The monastic life of the imprisoned criminal is partially relieved by gifts from friends and relatives in the outside world and purchases from the Inmate Store. These legitimate channels for securing extra goods are, however, severely restricted

---

10 Cf. S. Kirsen Weinberg, "Aspects of the Prison's Social Structure," *American Journal of Sociology*, Vol. XLVII, No. 5, March 1942, pp. 717-726. As this article points out, guards and prisoners are both driven to elevate themselves and deprecate their opponents until they reach extreme positions.

by the custodians' regulations and the prisoners' lack of re-sources. The inmate, for example, is permitted to spend only $25 per month at the Inmate Store, as we have noted earlier, but even this limit is beyond the reach of most prisoners—the actual expenditure is, on the average, less than $7 per month. The illegitimate channel for securing extra goods, that is, the looting of institutional supplies, is helpful, but it too has obvious defects. The society of captives cannot appreciably improve its material level of existence by wringing additional supplies from its environment, either rightfully or wrongfully.

But if the society of captives cannot improve its lot as a whole, it is possible for an individual prisoner to monopolize the scarce goods possessed by the society, to wrest from his fellow captives their few possessions, and thus soften the hurt of his material deprivation. In the argot of the inmates, an individual who takes what he wants from others by force is known as a *gorilla*. His is a satrapy based on violence and he preys on weaker or more fearful inmates in the cellblock, the industrial shops, or the recreation yard.

Now in many cases the actual use of force is unnecessary for the *gorilla*, for the mere threat of it in the background is sufficient to gain his ends. Unlike the custodians—who are barred from acts of brutality, attuned to the dangers of disorder, and in search of complex patterns of compliance—the man who plays the role of *gorilla* finds coercion or the threat of coercion a potent weapon. He stands ready to use a knife or a piece of pipe, he faces a lone victim, and his demands are simple. And it is this blatant readiness for the instrumental use of violence that often sets the *gorilla* off from other inmates rather than his strength, size or constant use of force. The threatened prisoner has the choice of submitting or fighting and like many others before him he may find discretion the better part of valor. Cigarettes, food, clothing, gestures of deference—all may flow to the man with a reputation for coercive exploitation once he has established his position in the pecking order which organizes much of the interaction among prisoners.

91

The prevalence of violence as a means of exploitation is far from new in the New Jersey State Prison—the first investigation of the institution in 1830 indignantly noted the existence of a "Stauch-Gang," a clique of rebellious inmates which intimidated fellow prisoners, cowed the guards, and busily devised numerous plans for escape.[11] At the present time, however, cliques of *gorillas*, in the sense of well organized and closely knit gangs of men who exploit other inmates by force, have largely disappeared. The *gorilla* of today tends to remain relatively isolated from the bonds of friendship, either because of preference or because he is rejected by other inmates; and if he attempts to form an alliance with other *gorillas*, not on the diffuse basis of friendship but on a narrow calculation of mutual advantage, the current custodial bureaucracy has learned how to cope with his efforts by means of solitary confinement and transfers to other institutions. Yet if there are few cliques at the present time—and these few are but loosely held together and small in size, consisting, perhaps, of a dominant figure and several sycophants—an association of coercive exploiters still poses a fearful threat for the general inmate population: As one prisoner has said, "If you decide to fight one of them you have to fight them all." It is, incidentally, the prevalence of *gorillas* in the prison which partially accounts for the weapons so frequently discovered in the officials' routine searches and surprise raids—the sliver of tin, the razor blade strapped to a toothbrush, the nail inserted in the melted end of a plastic fountain pen. These, as often as not, are seen by the inmates as their last means of defense in a world where the assaults of fellow prisoners are a greater danger than the barbarities of the captors.

The inmate who uses force, then, to gain the amenities of life may find himself in a hazardous position if he drives his victim too far or picks the wrong man to victimize, as a number of would-be *gorillas* have discovered to their sorrow. And, indeed, there is a widespread belief in the inmate population

[11] See Harry Elmer Barnes, *A History of the Penal, Reformatory, and Correctional Institutions of the State of New Jersey*, Trenton, New Jersey: MacCrellish & Quigley Company, 1918, p. 75.

that most *gorillas* are cowards and that tactics of coercion are successful only because the man who lets himself be coerced is somewhat more cowardly than the man who coerces him. In the harsh logic of the prison, the inmate who submits is a *weakling*. "You put a little pressure on a *weakling*," a prisoner has explained, "and he can't take it. You push him into a corner and put a knife against him and he begins to squeal." Be that as it may, there are a number of prisoners who avoid violence as a means of exploitation and turn to manipulating other inmates instead.

A portion of manipulative exploitation in the prison consists of outright fraud and chicanery, such as a simple failure to carry out a bargain in the exchange of goods and services, cheating on gambling debts, and so on. And on occasion fraud can be a more elaborate affair, as when one inmate, working in the Center as a sweeper and gaining access to the plans of the officials, was able to cozen his fellow prisoners into believing that he had great influence with the custodians. But as a manipulative mode of adjustment to the rigors of imprisonment, these swindles are overshadowed by the act of selling itself. Confronted by the facts of their material deprivation, the inmates have drawn a sharp line between selling and giving and the prisoner who sells when he should give is labelled a *merchant* or *pedlar*.

Now it is true, of course, that a balanced reciprocity of gifts functions much like a system of barter and that in the prison, as elsewhere, openhanded generosity is apt to be strained by the "free loader," the man who neglects the principle of equivalence, thus underlining the barter aspect of "giving." Yet as Hoebel has pointed out, the exchange of gifts is something more than a disguised version of utilitarian economics. Giving, as opposed to selling for profit, expresses the solidarity of the group and may, indeed, strengthen the social bonds among group members as contractual barter never can.[12] It is in this light that the inmate population views the *merchant* or *ped-*

[12] For a discussion of the non-economic aspects of exchange, see E. Adamson Hoebel, *Man in the Primitive World*, New York: McGraw-Hill Book Company, 1949, pp. 346-347.

93

lar, for he is defined as a man so alienated from other prisoners, so selfish in his pursuit of material advantage, that he is willing to thrive on the misery of his companions. In short, he places his own well-being above the well-being of the inmates as a whole. He does not share the goods in short supply but exploits, instead, the need of others.[13]

There are, to be sure, limits placed on the demands for generosity in the inmate population. *Rats, center men, weaklings,* and other figures held in hatred or contempt lie outside the pale and close friends possess a stronger claim than the newly arrived prisoner—the *fish*—or the relative stranger from another cellblock. And the inmates tend to distinguish between gifts from the free community and goods purchased from the inmate store, on the one hand, and material stolen from the institution's supplies, on the other. The former are, in a sense, the prisoner's private possessions and if the prisoner chooses to sell them it is perhaps "understandable" or "excusable" although the practice is not admired. But to sell material that has been filched from the officials is beyond the bounds of condoning, for, in the words of an inmate, "The man stealing stuff from the institution is stealing from me. He shouldn't try and sell it to me." This is quite literally true in the case of food stolen from the supplies for the inmates' messhall and is true to some extent in other areas as well; and thus there is some tendency for two classes of goods to exist in the prison. In general, however, the generosity of giving or sharing the amenities of life so treasured by the captive population—the cigarettes, the candy, the extra food or clothing, the material to decorate a cell, or the homemade liquor manufactured from fruit juice and rye bread—is normatively demanded by the inmate code, regardless of the source of the goods or the closeness of the bond with the prisoner in want; and the following description of one inmate, given by another, was expressed in the accents of deepest praise:

13 Cigarettes are the major medium of exchange in the New Jersey State Prison, as is the case in many custodial institutions in the United States.

94

"My cell partner—he can't say no. He'll have a can of milk. And he knows he ain't going to get no more milk until the next store order. And a complete stranger will come along and say 'I ain't got no milk' and he'll give it to him. Or cigarettes, the same way. And a couple of weeks later, the guy will come back and he'll *still* give him cigarettes. He's the kind of guy who'd give you the shirt off his back, if you know what I mean."

The *merchant* or *pedlar*, then, violates this ideal of liberality and is despised as a consequence—not simply because he often drives a hard bargain but also because his impersonal dealings are a denial of the unity of imprisoned criminals. He, like the *gorilla*, treats his fellow captives as objects rather than as persons; and if his tactics of exploitation involve manipulation rather than coercion, his behavior is no less destructive of the solidarity of the rejected.

Wolves, Punks, and Fags

The inmates of the New Jersey State Prison recognize and label a variety of homosexual acts, such as sodomy, fellatio, transvestism, frottage, and so on, although the labels of the inmates are not those of the medical profession or modern psychiatry. And the inmates, too, attempt to distinguish the "true" sexual pervert and the prisoner driven to homosexuality by his temporary deprivation.[14] In the world of the prison, however, the extent to which homosexual behavior involves "masculinity" and "femininity" would appear to override all other considerations and it is this which provides the main basis for the classification of sexual perversion by the inmate population. Homosexuals are divided into those who play an active, aggressive role, i.e. a "masculine" role by the stern standards of the prisoners, and those who play a more passive

---

[14] Cf. W. Norwood East, "Sexual Offenders," in *Mental Abnormality and Crime*, edited by L. Radzinowicz and J. W. C. Turner, London: Macmillan and Co., 1948, p. 186: "It is convenient to regard a true sexual perversion as sexual activity in which complete satisfaction is sought and obtained without the necessity of heterosexual intercourse. It must be persistently indulged in, preferably in reality, at any rate in phantasy, and must not be merely a substitute for a preferred heterosexual activity which, for some environmental reason, is difficult to obtain."

and submissive part. The former are termed *wolves*; the latter are referred to as *punks* and *fags*.

Now it is true that the society of captives does draw a line between *punks* and *fags*. "*Punks*," it is said, "are made, but *fags* are born." And in this curt aphorism the inmates are pointing to a difference between those who engage in homosexuality because they are coerced into doing so or because male prostitution is a means of winning goods and services in short supply and those who engage in homosexuality because it is preferred. But this division of passive homosexual roles on the basis of motive or genesis is accompanied by—and overshadowed by—the idea that *punks* and *fags* differ in the kind of femininity involved in their sexual aberration. The *fag*—the man who engages in homosexuality because "he likes it" or because "he wants to," according to the prisoners—is a man with a womanly walk and too-graceful gestures; he may, on occasion, dye his underclothing, curl his hair, or color his lips with homemade lipstick. As one inmate, much given to thoughtful analysis, has explained, "The *fag* is recognizable by his exaggerated, feminine mannerisms. The *fag*—they call him a *queen* on the West Coast—employs the many guiles for which females are noted, like playing 'stay away closer' or 'hard to get but gettable.'" The *fag*, in short, fills the stereotype of the homosexual as it is commonly held in the free community. He has forfeited his claim to masculinity not only by his reversal of the sexual role per se but also by taking on the outward guise of women.

The *punk*, on the other hand, submits to the importunities of the more active, aggressive homosexuals without displaying the outward signs of femininity in other aspects of his behavior. His forfeiture of masculinity is limited to the homosexual act. But even though the *punk* does not exhibit those mannerisms characterized as feminine by the inmate population, he has turned himself into a woman, in the eyes of the prisoners, by the very act of his submission. His is an inner softness or weakness; and, from the viewpoint of the prisoners, his sacrifice of manhood is perhaps more contemptible than that of the *fag* because he acts from fear or for the sake of quick advantage rather than personal inclination. In the words of the inmate quoted above, "A *punk* can't fend off the pressure of older, tougher men who may have bullied him, grilled him, put the arm on him in some other institution. He's basically morally weak to begin with, but because he has no source of finances the older, tougher cons ply him with cigarettes, candy, extra food supplies, and maybe even hooch. The weaker ones usually make a deliberate trade, but in some cases the kid may be told that he's not getting it for nothing. He's told he's got to pay up and since he hasn't got the money he's given an alternative—he'll get beaten up or he'll have to submit to an unnatural act. *Punks* are cowards."

The society of captives, then, distinguishes between *punks* and *fags* partly on the basis of differences in the causes or origins of their passive homosexuality. But, more importantly, both *punks* and *fags* fail to be men—the former because they lack an inner core of "toughness" and the latter because they assume the overt, obvious symbols of womanhood. Both are set off from the more active, aggressive, "masculine" *wolf*.

The stress on the "masculinity" of the *wolf's* role is reinforced by the fact that many inmates believe his part in a homosexual relationship to be little more than a search for a casual, mechanical act of physical release. Unmoved by love, indifferent to the emotions of the partner he has coerced, bribed, or seduced into a liaison, the *wolf* is often viewed as simply masturbating with another person. By thus stripping the *wolf* of any aura of "softness," of sentiment or affection, his homosexuality loses much of the taint of effeminacy which homosexuality often carries in the free community. His perversion is a form of rape and his victim happens to be a man rather than a woman, due to the force of circumstances.

It would appear, therefore, that the inmates of the New Jersey State Prison have changed the criteria by which an individual establishes his claim to the status of male. Shut off from the world of women, the population of prisoners finds itself unable to employ that criterion of maleness which looms

97

so importantly in society at large—namely, the act of hetero-sexual intercourse itself. Proof of maleness, both for the self and for others, has been shifted to other grounds and the display of "toughness," in the form of masculine mannerisms and the demonstration of inward stamina, now becomes the major route to manhood. These are used by the society at large, it is true; but the prison, unlike the society at large, must rely on them exclusively. In short, there are primary and secondary sexual characteristics in terms of social behavior just as there are primary and secondary sexual characteristics in terms of biological attributes; and the inmates have been forced to fall back on the secondary proof of manhood in the area of personal relations, i.e. "toughness," since the primary proof, in the form of heterosexual intercourse, is denied them. And the reliance on the secondary proof of manhood is so great that the active, aggressive homosexual—the *wolf*—almost manages to escape the stigma of his perversion.

By the standards of the free community, the prisoners' definition of masculine behavior may seem excessive with its emphasis on callousness, its flinty indifference to the more tender aspects of human relationships. It is perhaps understandable, however, in light of the fact that the definition of masculine behavior in a society composed exclusively of men is apt to move to an extreme position. But more important for our present analysis is the fact that by changing the criteria of maleness, the prisoners have erected a defense against the threat posed by their involuntary celibacy. The path to manhood has been reopened. However difficult to achieve or however harsh its mode of expression, "toughness"—and thus manhood—is at least possible. The anxieties generated by isolation from women and homosexuality lose something of their sting, since the individual's conception of himself as a male no longer depends so completely on his sexual activity. The *fag* and the *punk* must, of course, still bear the burden of the "softness" and the *wolf*—no matter how "tough" he may be—cannot entirely avoid the attitudes commonly elicited by his perversion. But for homosexuals and non-homosexuals

98

alike, the emphasis placed by the society of captives on the accompaniments of sexuality rather than sexuality itself does much to transform the problem of being a man in a world without women.

Ball Busters and Real Men

A group of oppressed men may revolt even if their revolt is almost certain to fail, as we have pointed out before, and the same thing may be said of an individual. Fully aware that the custodians hold the upper hand in the last analysis, knowing that solitary confinement awaits the inmate who angers the guards beyond the point of endurance, there are some prisoners who none the less flare into open defiance. Such men are labelled *ball busters* in the argot of the captives, for as one inmate has said, "That kind of a con is always giving the screws a hard time." Blatant disobedience, physical and verbal assaults on the officials, the constant creation of disturbances—these are the patterns of behavior of the typical *ball buster* and the following inmate's account is a fair illustration:

"I was sitting in that window yesterday and the officer came over to me, he talked to me like a dog. I said, 'Look, I've got a stripe on my britches and a number on my back, but don't forget this. I'm a man.' I said, 'To you, to you, and to you, and to the warden out there in the Front House and to everyone else in this institution or in this world, I'm a man.' I said, 'I want to be treated as such and not anything else.' He talked to me like a dog. He said, 'Get out of that God damned window.' I told him, 'I have permission to sit here. The warden has said it's alright to sit here. I shall continue to sit here. I have been sitting here for seven years and if I'm here seven more years, I'll still be sitting here. I was here before you came and I'll most likely be here when you go. I've got to live here, I've got to put up with it, but I don't have to put up with you.' "

Now as one writer has pointed out, such men possess a certain Promethean quality.[15] They have, in effect, refused to come to terms with their helplessness, their loss of autonomy,

[15] Richard McCleery, "Institutional Change: A Case Study of Prison Management in Transition, 1945-1955," unpublished Ph.D. dissertation, University of North Carolina, 1956.

and they continue to shout their defiance despite the ultimate hopelessness of their position. And it might seem that such men would win the admiration and approval of their fellow prisoners, since they voice the imprisoned criminal's hostility against officialdom. Weak, dependent, and chafed by a thousand restrictive regulations, the inmate population might be expected to see the figure of the *ball buster* as a welcome symbol of courageous opposition. In fact, however, this is only partially true, for the *ball buster* is often regarded as a fool. He disturbs that delicate system of compromise and corruption which the prisoners have established with their guards—in the words of the inmates, "He keeps things all shook up." Stricter surveillance, further restrictions, and the alienation of the guardians all flow from his useless, individualistic insurrection. He has sacrificed the well being of the inmate population as a whole for the sake of a childish, emotional outburst and his fellow inmates view him with contempt. If the *ball buster* has good grounds for his rebellion—if he has been goaded beyond endurance by the standards of the prison world—he may avoid the disparagement of other inmates, particularly if he acts with a cool calculation of the personal consequences rather than with frenzied anger. In general, however, the man who fights back is a man who is viewed as a troublemaker, not only by the guards but by the inmates as well. "A guy who goes out of his way to antagonize an officer," as one prisoner tersely said, "gets all the inmates into a jam. And besides, he's an idiot. He's the sort of person who'll come up and ask you for a stamp when you're washing your hands."

In the Prison, then, the open mutiny of a single inmate against the power of the custodians is frequently defined not as an act of heroism but as a thoughtless loss of self control which calls down the wrath of the rulers. As a result, the role of *ball buster* in the inmate social system is apt to carry little prestige.[16] Instead, the man who can "take it," who can endure

---

[16] It is true that there are some inmates in the New Jersey State Prison for whom "giving the *screws* a hard time" appears to rank as a dominant value. These men, however, are more than likely to be sentenced to solitary

the regime of the custodians without flinching, is the man who wins the admiration and respect of his fellow captives.

The ideal of fortitude is, at first glance, the counsel of despair, for it bids us endure that which cannot be avoided. In the prison, however, emphasis is placed not on simple acceptance but on dignity and composure under stress and these are at least partially subject to the individual's control. The rigors of the inmate's world are to be met with a certain self-containment and the excessive display of emotion is to be avoided at all costs. The prisoner should speak slowly and deliberately and he should move in the same fashion. Curiosity, anxiety, surprise—all are to be carefully curbed. Even too great a show of humor must be checked since there is the danger of being thought a clown or a buffon. The prisoner, in short, is urged to "play it cool," to control all affect in a hard, silent stoicism which finds its apotheosis in the legendary figure of the cowboy or the gangster.[17]

Now it is clear that this concept of fortitude has its roots in a vision of manhood and integrity which far transcends the prison. Self-restraint, reserve, taciturnity, and emotional balance have long been the virtues of the hero in a variety of cultural traditions and they are virtues which feed on adversity. The prisoner who can "take it" plays a part in a drama far older than the custodial institution for the convicted criminal and the value placed on endurance does not simply depend on the conditions of confinement. And it is also clear that the inmate population's view of fortitude as an ideal involves a kind of "toughness" which is linked to the masculine mannerisms and inward stamina so important in the area of sexual activities. The important point, however, is that the society of captives has institutionalized the virtue of dignity —the ability to "take it," to maintain the self—in a series of norms and reinforced these norms with a variety of informal

---

confinement and thus their influence on the general inmate population tends to be reduced.

[17] See, for example, Robert Warshow, "The Gangster as Tragic Hero," *Partisan Review*, Vol. xv, No. 2, February 1948, pp. 240-244.

social controls. Deprived of their autonomy by the extensive rules of the custodians' regime, the inmates of the New Jersey State Prison have shifted the measure of the individual's worth from rebellion to adjustment. Thus it is not the futile and disturbing defiance of the *ball buster* that is accorded approbation; rather, it is the mute strength to maintain some degree of personal integration.

There is no single, fixed term for the inmate who endures the rigors of imprisonment with dignity, but the label of *real man* is applied, I think, as frequently as any other. The *real man* is a prisoner who "pulls his own time" in the phrasing of the inmate population and he confronts his captors with neither subservience nor aggression. Somewhat aloof, seldom complaining, he embodies the inmates' version of decorum. And if the *real man's* efforts to maintain his integrity in the face of privation have an important psychological utility—for the *real man* regains his autonomy, in a sense, by denying the custodians' power to strip him of his ability to control himself—it is also true that his role is of vital functional significance for the social system of imprisoned criminals. In the emphasis on endurance with dignity, the inmates have robbed the rebel of their support; it is the man who can stop himself from striking back at the custodians that wins their admiration and thus their image of the hero functions wittingly or unwittingly to maintain the *status quo*.

Toughs and Hipsters

It is clear that violence runs like a bright thread through the fabric of life in the New Jersey State Prison and no inmate can afford to ignore its presence. We have spoken of the calculated use of violence in the role of the *gorilla* and the *wolf*; in these we have the employment of violence or the threat of violence for the sake of winning material benefits or sexual favors. And we have spoken of the emotional violence of the *ball buster* who plunges into revolt against the guards. There remains, however, another form of violence which is no less disruptive for the society of captives, namely the violence of the inmate who is quick to quarrel with his fellow prisoners. His assaults flow from the fact that he feels he has been insulted rather than a desire to exploit others and his violence is directed against his companions in misery rather than against the custodians. The inmate population carefully notes the nature of his outbursts and labels him a *tough*. Frequently fighting with a certain cold ferocity and swift to seek revenge for the slightest affront, the *tough* is regarded by other inmates with a curious mixture of fear and respect.

The reason for fearing the *tough* is plain enough. He is marked by a "touchiness" which makes every encounter with him hazardous and he poses a constant danger for the society of captives jammed together in an involuntary community of stone and steel. But on what grounds can he be accorded prestige? It seems paradoxical that the *tough*—the man who explodes into violence directed against fellow prisoners—should be respected, while the *ball buster*—the man who directs his aggression against the officials—is apt to be regarded with contempt. Both the *tough* and the *ball buster* are disruptive forces in the life of the prison and both would appear to lack the self-control which forms such an important basis for the prestige of the *real man*. A part of the answer lies in the fact that some of the respect paid to the *tough* represents the deference of terror, for the *tough*, unlike the *ball buster*, confronts other inmates with the direct and immediate threat of a physical assault. He is a person to be placated and manipulated with homage. Even more importantly, however, the *tough* exhibits the active, aggressive "masculinity" so valued by inmates and he is defined as possessing a raw courage which compensates for his instability. In fact, the prisoners see the *tough's* violence not so much as a matter of wild anger but as cold retaliation and he is slightly more ready to detect a slight than most. The *tough* is not a bully, for he will fight with anyone, the strong as well as the weak. "He won't take anything from anybody," say the prisoners and if the *tough* threatens the personal security of other inmates he also stands prepared to forfeit his own. Thus his vices are his virtues and

103

the inmate population cannot fail to view him with some ambivalence. He is a *real man* turned sour, in a sense, and he has transformed his inward strength from the ability to take it to the ability to hand it out.

The role of the *tough* is obviously based on some rather finely drawn distinctions, particularly in the area of physical courage. For the inmates of the New Jersey State Prison, however, violence is a familiar companion rather than a rare breach in social relationships and they are keenly aware of its different meanings. The prisoners draw a firm line between violence which stems from "real" courage and violence which is part of a pattern of braggadocio. The inmate who pretends to be "tougher than he really is," who "shoots off his mouth" and chooses the victim of his aggression with caution, is singled out and labelled a *hipster*.

This pretence of the *hipster* that identifies him in the eyes of the prisoners—this tendency to erect a false front—is seen as reaching far beyond a simulated bravery. "He wants to be a part of a group that he doesn't belong to," one prisoner has said in describing the man who plays the role of a *hipster*. "He's always trying to belong to that group and emulating them. He'll hear some fellows saying, 'Hey, did you read so and so? Yeh, that was good wasn't it?' He'll try and get that book so he can tell them, 'Yeh, I read it. It was a good book, wasn't it?' He wants to be like them. He wants to read the things they read, so he can discuss the things they discuss. He sees them lifting weights, he wants to go out there and lift weights. If he sees them out there playing handball, he wants to play handball. He wants to be part of them. But it's not a natural desire for him to read a certain book, or to act in a certain manner, or to strut around, or to talk out of the side of his mouth. Those things are put on. They are put on by those people we call *hipsters*."

Nonetheless, the major distinguishing characteristic of the *hipster* remains centered on the fact that he is, as another inmate has said, "the bully type—all wind and gum drops."

He lays claim to a greater courage than he possesses in fact and his show of toughness, whether assumed to ingratiate himself in his own eyes or in the eyes of others idealizing toughness, remains simply a façade.

Now the *tough* has met the problem of personal insecurity in the prison not by ignoring the irritants of daily life but by reacting to them with violence; *he* is the problem of personal insecurity from the point of view of many prisoners and his reputation tends to keep others at a distance. Instead of banding together with other inmates and holding group harmony as a value to be advanced at all costs, he follows the individualistic path of depending on his own strength and courage to settle the quarrels in which he becomes involved. Thus he frees himself to some extent from the depredations of the *gorilla* and the *wolf*, for he is a person to be approached with considerable prudence, and many inmates take pains not to give him cause for assault. The solution of the *tough* is far from perfect, however, for there are other *toughs* in the prison who are at least equally ready to fight; and some *hipsters*, intent on building a reputation for toughness, may deliberately provoke him in the belief that he can be beaten.[18]

Quick to anger, then, and slow to cool off, the prisoner addicted to "expressive" rather than "instrumental" violence intensifies the problems of the inmate population as a whole; and he himself, despite his momentary victories, stands as an invitation to further violence. He wins a measure of respect, it is true, but it is the respect of the brutalized and it is apt to reach no further than his fists. It is the *tough* and the *hipster* as much as any other who convert the prison into what one inmate has described as a gigantic playground—a place where blustering and brawling push life in the direction of a state of anomy.

18 In so far as the *hipster* can convince others that he is *possibly* dangerous, he also may be treated with a good deal of caution and deference, particularly by more fearful inmates. But the *hipster*, even more than the *tough*, is likely to be "tested" to see if he is bluffing.

III

I have presented the patterns of behavior distinguished and named by the inmates of the New Jersey State Prison with a greater simplicity than exists in reality. Argot roles are in fact generalized behavioral tendencies and the playing of a particular role by a particular prisoner is often a matter of degree. Furthermore, some inmates may play one role in the industrial shops, let us say, and another role in the Wing. A prisoner may quickly assume one role on first entering the institution and then shift to another role at a later point in time. But this is simply to reaffirm that the patterns of behavior which I have described are social roles rather than personality traits and that we are interested in the behavior of inmates as a system of action rather than as a collection of individual characteristics. *It is the structure of social relationships formed by imprisoned criminals which concerns us; an inmate may enter these relationships in a variety of capacities for varying periods of time, but it is the structure itself which lays the main claim on our attention.*

I have suggested that the main outlines of this structure, this system of action, are to be found in the inmate behavior patterns classified and named by the prisoners in light of the major problems which confront them. These major problems are, I have argued, five in number and involve deprivation or frustration in the areas of social acceptance, material possessions, heterosexual relationships, personal autonomy, and personal security. From the viewpoint of particular inmates, some of these problems may bite more deeply than others, but in general these problems constitute a common set of pains or rigors of confinement to which almost all prisoners must respond or adapt themselves.

Now the argot terms presented in this chapter largely refer to what I have chosen to call "alienative" modes of response to the specific problems posed by imprisonment. The *rat*, the *center man*, the *wolf*, the *punk*, the *fag*, the *gorilla*, the *merchant*, the *ball buster*, *tough*, and the *hipster*—all are social roles in which, generally speaking, the inmate attempts to reduce the rigors of prison life at the expense of fellow prisoners and the individual pursues his own interests, his own needs, without regard for the needs, rights, and opinions of others. Inmate cohesion or inmate solidarity is sacrificed for personal aggrandizement; bonds of mutual loyalty, aid, affection, and respect are subordinated to individualistic ends. The variety of "cohesive" responses to the pains of imprisonment, on the other hand, tend to be lumped together under the label of the *real man*, for this term is often extended to cover social roles which involve loyalty, generosity, sexual restraint, and the minimizing of frictions among inmates as well as endurance with dignity. The *real man* appears to form a central cluster of admired behavior patterns from which various types of deviance are measured and the label of *real man* provides a general antonym for the argot terms applied to "alienative" behavior patterns. In any case, it is clear that "cohesive" responses to the harsh conditions of prison life are to be found in the society of captives as well as "alienative" responses, even if prisoners fail to attach distinctive argot terms to each species of the former. *And the greater the extent of "cohesive" responses—the greater the degree to which the society of captives moves in the direction of inmate solidarity—the greater is the likelihood that the pains of imprisonment will be rendered less severe for the inmate population as a whole.* The deprivations and frustrations of prison life cannot be eliminated, it is true, but their consequences can be partially neutralized. A cohesive inmate society provides the prisoner with a meaningful social group with which he can identify himself and which will support him in his battles against his condemners—and thus the prisoner can at least in part escape the fearful isolation of the convicted offender. Inmate solidarity, in the form of mutual toleration, helps to solve the problems of personal security posed by the involuntary intimacy of men who are noteworthy for their seriously antisocial behavior in the past. Inmate solidarity, in the form of "sharing" or a reciprocity of gifts and favors, attacks one of the most potent sources of aggression among prisoners, the drive for material betterment by means of force and fraud. It is true

107

that goods in scarce supply will remain scarce even if they are shared rather than monopolized; but scarce goods will at least be distributed more equitably in a social system marked by solidarity and this may be of profound significance in enabling the prisoner to better endure the psychological burden of impoverishment. And a cohesive population of prisoners provides a system of shared, group-supported beliefs and values which will tend to curb forms of behavior such as sexual perversion, useless insurrections which bring only retaliation, and so on.

On the other hand, as the population of prisoners moves in the direction of a warring aggregate the many problems of prison life become more acute. If a war of all against all is apt to make life "solitary, poor, nasty, brutish, and short" for men with freedom, as Hobbes suggested, it would seem to be doubly true for men in custody. Even those who are most successful in exploiting their fellow prisoners will find it a dangerous and nerve-wracking game, for they cannot escape the company of their victims. And in so far as social rejection is a fundamental problem, a state of complete mutual alienation is worse than useless as a solution to the threats created by the inmate's status as an outcast.

The balance struck between the theoretical extremes of perfect solidarity and a war of all against all is, then, of vital significance—not only to the prison officials but to the inmates as well. This balance point, however, is not fixed. Rather, it represents a compromise of a host of competing forces which change through time and thus the structure of social relationships formed by imprisoned criminals is in a constant state of flux. These shifts in the balance point between cohesion and alienation among inmates are in turn part of a larger series of changes embracing the prison as a whole. In short, the social system of the New Jersey State Prison, like every social system, is marked by social change and it is only by examining the nature of this change that we can come to a full understanding of the society of captives.

CHAPTER SIX

CRISIS AND EQUILIBRIUM

THE CONCEPT OF CRISIS is frequently viewed as the antithesis of the concept of organization. Crisis represents the unexpected or disorderly whereas organization represents the anticipated or the routine. Crisis stands for abrupt shifts and hurried action. Organization stands for gradual change after long planning. Yet in some ways organization is simply a series of crises held within limits, a series of disorders which do not become too disorderly. Routine may be simply an ideal around which actual behavior fluctuates. The emergency, then, is a phase to be passed through again and again; and organization is many of these emergencies, these crises, tied together in a recognizable continuity.

The most dramatic crises of the prison are undoubtedly riots, although there are many other emergencies which disrupt this society within a society. The excitement and disturbance of an execution, the arrival of a famous racketeer, the granting of a pardon, a fight among the guards—all are outside the supposed habitual round of events. And many habitual activities, such as the daily mass movement of inmates, often evoke a crisis mood. The creation of a "critical mass," i.e. a large number of criminals freed from their cells and gathered in one place, is viewed as potential disaster. But riots remain the most striking of all the unexpected events, for they represent a complete and public denial of one of the most fundamental premises on which the prison is built, namely, that the officials, the surrogates of the free community, stand in unquestioned power over the inmates.

Now whatever may be the immediate drama of riots, such events have a long-range influence on the structure of the prison and they can leave their imprint on the society of captives in a variety of ways. If the warden sacrifices guards held hostage for the sake of a quick and forceful victory, the morale of the custodial force may be seriously impaired for a long time to come. Division within the inmate population may become obvious as the rebellion drags toward a settlement, creating permanent factions among the prisoners and forcing men into new roles. Relationships established by inmates with officials during a riot may serve as a sort of high water mark, a new boundary for future dealings. In short, insurrections do not end with the return of official control but become a part of the structure, like a flaw left in a piece of steel which has been subjected to excessive strain.

If riots, then, continue in a sense long after the public spectacle is done, we must also recognize that riots do not suddenly come into being but are a long time in the making. They are the culmination of a series of minor crises, each of which sets in motion forces for the creation of a new and more serious crisis. In other words, riots are not an "accident," an inexplicable, momentary flurry nor is the prison always a powder keg, as it is so commonly presented, waiting to be touched off by some chance spark. Instead, the prison appears to move in a cyclical rhythm from order to disorder to order; and riots—those most obvious, startling expressions of disorder—are a logical step in a pattern of repeated social change.

We do not mean to suggest that a cycle of riots and times of peace is an inevitable aspect of imprisonment. We would argue, however, that given the existing conditions of life in the maximum security institution, the social system of the prison is *not* what the economist would call a self-regulating or self-correcting mechanism in which disturbances to the equilibrium bring about changes which act to restore the original state of affairs. Rather, disturbances within the system tend to cause further disturbances which are apt to result in

110

a progressive departure from equilibrium.[1] But first let us examine some recent riots in the New Jersey State Prison in brief detail and see how they happen. Then, perhaps, we can better assess the place of riots in the prison's sequence of transformations through time.

II

It is often difficult to say whether or not a riot has occurred in the prison, for many revolts defined as a minor melée by the officials would probably be viewed by the free community as full-blown rebellions, if they were given more publicity. From the standpoint of the officials of the New Jersey State Prison, however, there is a vast difference between "flash disturbances" or "incidents" and riots; and the latter, in turn, are carefully distinguished on the basis of the number of inmates involved, the amount of planning, the presence or absence of hostages, and the apparent objectives of the rioters such as mass escape, organized protest, or the wild expression of hatred of men brought to the breaking point.

Nonetheless, both the officials and the free community would agree that the New Jersey State Prison experienced riots in the Spring of 1952. These outbursts, in fact, appear to have been part of a general wave of unrest which swept over custodial institutions in the United States between 1951 and 1953. Michigan, Louisiana, North Carolina, Idaho, Georgia, Kentucky, California, Massachusetts, Ohio, Illinois, Utah, New Mexico, Pennsylvania, Arizona, Washington, Oregon, Minnesota—all were confronted with uprisings within a span of three years.[2]

---

[1] From a long-range point of view, it is possible that the social system of the prison could be seen as a self-correcting mechanism in that the most serious disturbances set in motion forces which bring them to an end. (Cf. James Arthur Esty, *Business Cycles*, New York: Prentice-Hall, 1941, p. 126.) And it also should be noted that there are important stabilizing forces at work in the prison, even if they are insufficient to check the general drift of events. This will be treated at greater length later in the book.

[2] For an excellent, detailed account of the riots in Michigan's Jackson Prison, see John Bartlow Martin, *Break Down the Walls*, New York: Ballantine Books, 1954.

In the State Prison at Trenton, the first riot began slowly on the evening of Saturday, March 29, 1952. At 11:30 P.M., an inmate in the solidary confinement Wing complained of being ill to the guard on duty and asked him to call the doctor.[3] The guard telephoned the Center and the senior official in charge in turn telephoned the prison hospital, asking that an inmate orderly be sent to 5 Wing to check the prisoner's condition. According to official reports, at least, there was no delay. The orderly arrived, took the inmate's temperature, checked his pulse and respiration and noted his complaint—headache and running nose. The orderly then telephoned the resident physician and since the prisoner's temperature and pulse were within normal limits the doctor prescribed medication to be taken to the prisoner's cell.

The prisoner now began to groan and threw himself from his bunk to the floor. Several inmates in nearby cells started chanting, "Take that boy to the hospital, take that boy to the hospital. . . ." When the medicine arrived from the hospital, the prisoner refused to take it and continued to groan on the floor; and the noise level—that significant indicator of tension within the walls—rose sharply. The Wing guard again called the Center. He was told that orders are not to be changed because the inmates do not like them: The prisoner could not be taken to the hospital. Shouting and rattling spoons on the bars of their cells, the inmates of 5 Wing threatened to "take the joint apart" if the prisoner were not taken to the doctor.

At this point, the voice of one prisoner could be heard above the others. "If I start smashing things, will you go along with me?" He was answered by an encouraging chorus. Breaking the wash basin in his cell with the leg torn from the bed, he threw the pieces to the floor of the Wing and other inmates immediately followed his example.

Again the Wing guard called the Center and now the Center acted. An officer arrived, the cell of the complaining inmate was unlocked, and the inmate marched, still groaning in

[3] At that time 5 Wing served as a prison within a prison for the most troublesome offenders. In earlier years, before women were kept in a separate institution, 5 Wing had been used to house female prisoners.

112

apparent pain, to the hospital. The removal of the prisoner did not, however, quiet the disturbance but instead seemed to give it greater impetus. Thirty minutes later all the lights in the Wing had been smashed, missiles rained from the tiers to the cellblock floor, and the prisoners screamed at each other ever more loudly in the darkness. The guard desperately called the Center for new instructions, and he was ordered out of the Wing for his own protection. "He could do nothing in the dark against 52 rioting men," noted the official reports.

Shortly thereafter prisoners were seen at large in the Wing. The Center recalled all guards off duty to the prison and two shells of tear gas were shot into 5 Wing, but with little effect. The rioting continued. At noon the next day, however, according to the accounts of the prison officials, it became "apparent that the demonstration could not be successful." Twenty prisoners walked out of 5 Wing and gave themselves up and the remaining prisoners surrendered in the evening. They made no demands—they simply asked how they would be punished. The rioters were taken to the hospital, examined, and placed in solitary confinement in another cellblock to await further decision. As it turned out, no cause for action could be found for 45 of the prisoners from 5 Wing; they could not be positively identified as participating in the riot. The seven prisoners who could be identified as actively taking part in the disturbance were sentenced to 45 days in solitary confinement and then held indefinitely in seclusion to await further investigation.

What of the inmate who complained of being ill? He was not seriously sick, according to the doctor who examined him more thoroughly at the prison hospital; and it still remains unknown whether he acted on his own behalf or at the instigation of others who then took up his cause.

The second riot at the New Jersey State Prison was a far more serious affair in the eyes of the officials. There was, they say, evidence of careful planning and the storage of food supplies. Furthermore, the rioting prisoners managed to seize

113

hostages, thus introducing a new and much more disturbing note into the proceedings.

It began on Tuesday morning, April 15, 1952, in the Print Shop. A few inmates left the building shortly before the riot started, apparently aware of the impending uprising but unwilling to have a hand in it, while other prisoners hurried to the scene. At approximately 11:00 A.M. 69 prisoners in the Print Shop seized two guards and two shop instructors, barricaded the door, and marked the beginning of their rebellion with a wildly destructive spree: Later estimates placed the damage done to the machinery, tools, and supplies at $90,000. The prison officials quickly and quietly locked all other inmates in the institution in their cells. State Troopers, local police, and off-duty guards were hastily summoned, the two-story stone building which contained the Print Shop was surrounded, and water and electricity were shut off in preparation for a siege.

"There will be no bloodshed unless the guards force us out," announced the ringleader of the rioters on the second day. "We know we will have to leave sooner or later, but we're sacrificing for what we want. We're outlaws from the word go. We're the scum of society." Whatever may have been the feelings of the prison officials about this rather flamboyant, melodramatic statement (and it is to be noted that the rioters in the Print Shop demanded that newspapermen be present at all meetings with the officials), the necessity for discussing what the rioters wanted was all too clear. Members of officialdom were now held captive. The rioters could have been removed by force "in 10 minutes," the Warden later claimed, but he feared for the safety of the hostages. Brought to an apparent impasse, the officials opened negotiations with the inmates in the Print Shop and hoped for the best.

In the beginning, the rioters voiced many demands ranging from the Warden's discharge to the revision of parole procedures. The Commissioner of Institutions and Agencies countered with the proposal that a committee of seven men should be selected from the prison at large "to discuss complaints against the regime." The inmates in the Print Shop drank the water in the fire buckets, built fires to keep warm, fashioned weapons from the paper-cutting blades taken from a printing machine, and sent out a new list of demands. The Governor of New Jersey announced to the public that he had complete confidence in the Commissioner's handling of the situation and the Commissioner declared that he would stand by the Warden. The uprising entered its third day.

On the afternoon of Thursday, April 17, the State Prison Farm at Rahway flared into riot, seemingly, as one official said at the time, based on sympathy with the demonstrators at Trenton and a "general desire to raise hell."[4] Some 230 inmates seized 9 hostages, barricaded themselves in a dormitory, and surrendered five days later. The immediate effect of the Rahway riot on the rebellion at the Trenton Prison, however, was to rob the latter of much of its publicity and this well may have hastened the end of the affair. Weakened by thirst and hunger, the rioters in the Print Shop gave up the struggle on the afternoon of Friday, April 18, approximately 77 hours after the beginning of their revolt, and marched out two by two into the hands of the waiting guards. The hostages were released unharmed. (One guard, suffering a heart attack, had been released by the inmates on the previous day.) The rioting prisoners had managed to wring three concessions from their captors: First, that the New Jersey State Prison would be investigated by an impartial, independent agency; second, that no corporal punishment would be inflicted on the rioters; and third, that an inmate committee would be formed for the presentation of grievances.

---

[4] The penal institutions of New Jersey actually experienced five disturbances in 1952. The first—the riot in 5 Wing at the Maximum Security Prison on March 29—we have discussed. The second consisted of a brief effort by five inmates to break out of solitary confinement in the Maximum Security Prison on the night of April 5. The third incident—the so-called Print Shop riot—began, as we have noted, on April 15; and the fourth disturbance occurred at Rahway on April 17. The fifth took place on October 12 and centered on an escape attempt. As far as disturbances at the New Jersey State Prison itself are concerned, however, only the outbreaks of March 29 and April 15 are dignified by the officials with the name of riot.

The surrender of the inmates in the Print Shop touched off a flurry of letter writing. The Deputy Commissioner of the Division of Corrections submitted a list of the names of the men involved in the riot to the chairman of the State Parole Board. A letter was sent from the Commissioner of Institutions and Agencies to the Warden of the New Jersey State Prison requesting that idle men be put to work as soon as possible. Letters arrived at the prison from the NAACP asking for an investigation of complaints made by Negro inmates concerning discrimination within the walls. A member of the prison's classification board, described in a newspaper account as being completely lacking in institutional training or experience, indignantly denied the assertion in a letter to the senior officials of the prison. The Warden received a letter from an inmate demanding that he be reimbursed by the State for losses of personal property suffered during the disturbance. A note was sent from the Division of Corrections to the State Prosecutor stating that action in the courts against the rioters would be unwise, since it would simply furnish "irresponsible characters with another opportunity to make headlines by shouting extravagant charges in public." But in addition to this rush of correspondence, the New Jersey State Prison broke into activity in a number of other areas: Repairs for the physical damage left in the riot's wake were begun, hearings within the prison were started by an investigating committee appointed by the Governor of the State, and stringent security measures were imposed to forestall future insurrections. And, in accordance with the terms of surrender, an Inmate Council was formed for the presentation and discussion of grievances.

Consisting of seven prisoners elected by the general inmate population, the Inmate Council selected a chairman and a secretary from its members and met with the Warden on April 28; and shortly thereafter the Commissioner of the Department of Institutions and Agencies issued the following *Memorandum Confirming the Establishment of the Inmate Council of the New Jersey State Prison.*

It is believed that all concerned will benefit if cooperation between the inmates and the officials and employees of the New Jersey State Prison is facilitated by the establishment of regular and mutually accepted channels of communication whereby questions having to do with the welfare of the inmate body as a whole can be discussed and the inmates' recommendations made known to the officials.

To accomplish these aims, the establishment of a conference committee elected by all the inmates is confirmed and it is suggested that the name of the committee shall be the Inmate Council of the New Jersey State Prison.

The following rules are adopted to govern the relationships between the committee and the officials of the Department of Institutions and Agencies and the New Jersey State Prison:

1. The Council will be recognized as the duly elected representatives of the inmate body by the Commissioner of Institutions and Agencies, the Deputy Commissioner in Charge of Correction, the Board of Managers, and the Principal Keeper.

2. The members of the Council shall include one representative of each wing and one representative of the indeterminate group of the institution elected annually by ballot, and no member shall serve on the Council unless duly elected. A special election to unseat and replace a council member may be held upon presentation to the Principal Keeper of a petition signed by 60 percent of the residents of a wing. The administration will take no part in the selection of wing representatives, but an official or officials designated by the Principal Keeper will serve with a committee of the Inmate Council as election commissioners to insure that all elections are conducted properly and fairly.

3. It shall be the duty and responsibility of the Inmate Council to ascertain the opinions and recommendations of the inmate body with respect to matters pertaining to the general welfare of the inmates and to faithfully and accurately convey these opinions and recommendations to the chief administrative officer of the prison. The Council will not intercede with any official of the prison or the Department of Institutions and Agencies on behalf of an individual inmate.

4. So long as the Council and its members remain in good standing in the institution each member thereof shall have the privilege of interviewing any or all of the inmates in the group which he represents without surveillance of any employee. The Principal Keeper may, by reason of the bad conduct or segregation of any inmate, deny this privilege. It is intended by this

117

paragraph to permit personal interviews with inmates and admission to the various facilities of the institution.

5. It is to be understood that the Council will not be quoted as in favor of or opposed to any matter except by express approval of the Council as a whole. No person may therefore quote the Council without its approval.

6. Under conditions to be prescribed by the Principal Keeper, the Council may have access to the institutional radio system at reasonable times for the purpose of disseminating information to the inmates. This privilege can be withdrawn at any time by the Principal Keeper if abused.

7. Except in an emergency, major changes in policy and practices affecting the welfare of the inmates shall be taken up first with the Inmate Council. It is understood that the Principal Keeper may call upon the Council to correctly interpret any changes in policy or practice and to assist in implementing such changes.

8. It will be understood that at a specific time each day an authorized representative of the Council may, if there are matters to be presented, confer with the Principal Keeper or an official designated by him. It is understood that any matters referred by the Council to the administration will be handled and decided as rapidly as possible.

9. Major proposals and resolutions by the entire Council shall be in writing. All replies shall likewise be in writing.

10. Every official in the institution will be instructed to cooperate to the full with the Council.

11. It is hoped and expected that by this method the method may be supplied whereby complaints and grievances may be promptly presented and disposed of. It is not to be expected that such requests can be granted if in the judgement of the Principal Keeper they shall interfere with the maintenance of a necessary and humane discipline in the institution.

12. It would be advisable, at least in the early stages of its activities, that the Council meet with the officials on a date mutually agreed upon with the presence of the Principal Keeper and the Commissioner or his Deputy. It would be advisable to have a monthly report prepared by the Council and forwarded to the officials.

13. The Principal Keeper is by law vested with complete authority in the management of the institution and the maintenance of discipline; and nothing contained in this agreement is to be inconsistent with that legal obligation.

14. This arrangement shall be terminated whenever in the judgement of the Commissioner and the Principal Keeper it has

ceased to serve a useful purpose or to facilitate that cooperation between the employees and inmates so essential to the satisfactory operation of the institution.

At the first meeting of the Inmate Council and the Governor's Committee to investigate the prison, the inmates insisted that two prisoners who had not been elected to the Council but who had large personal followings in the institution should be present at all future discussions. One of these prisoners was, in fact, the acknowledged leader of the Print Shop riot and the Governor's Committee felt some qualms about the propriety of his inclusion. It was decided, however, that he should be permitted to attend the meetings and he was subsequently elected as a delegate-at-large to the Inmate Council.

In their conferences with the prison officials and the members of the Department of Institutions and Agencies, the inmates presented a list of complaints ranging from the lack of funds for eyeglasses, dentures, and so forth for indigent convicts to the number of men kept idle. The custodians attempted to answer the grievances and requests of the prisoners in what appears to be a straightforward and sincere fashion and they carefully pointed out the remedies planned, the changes under way, and insurmountable barriers to certain proposals. Between May 12 and May 28, however, the relationships between the Inmate Council and the prison administrators began to deteriorate rapidly. The prisoners pressed for a number of innovations—such as an increase in the number of delegates-at-large, the duty and obligation of the Inmate Council to intercede with the prison officials on the behalf of individual inmates, the visiting of inmates in solitary confinement, and the holding of Inmate Council meetings at the discretion of the chairman—which the custodians viewed as an intolerable encroachment on their powers. When these demands were denied, the Inmate Council staged a sit-down strike for five days in the room in the Front House which the officials had supplied for the Council's conferences; and it was during this period that the inmates' delegate-at-large, the

119

prisoner who had led the Print Shop riot, was elected chairman. From that time on, said the Commissioner of the Department of Institutions and Agencies, "all relations with the Council deteriorated as a result of his loud, boisterous, rebellious attitude."

On July 14 and 15 the prison officials seized the chairman of the Inmate Council and his followers and transferred them to county jails in New Brunswick, Trenton, and Woodbury. The Inmate Council was never officially disbanded, according to the Commissioner, but it ceased to play a significant role in the life of the prison. Thus ended the effort of the captives to secure a voice in the determination of the regime of the New Jersey State Prison and the institution moved in the direction of "normalcy." The custodians had regained control.

III

Who was to blame for the riots? In this question the free community expressed its indignation and anxiety, for a riot is the imprisoned criminal brought back to life, the marked man revealed again to the public view. A riot is not one criminal tried in court, unknown, unnoticed, and then quietly placed behind the wall. A riot, rather, is a disturbing reminder of society's decision to punish some to protect the many and simultaneously records the failure of penal policy. The imprisoned criminal, unreformed, has gained the upper hand; and the free community responds by searching for a personal villain in the piece.

Riots are of course a political issue, embarrassing to the party in office. Thus for some the individual responsible for the insurrections in the New Jersey State Prison was not hard to find, as indicated in the following newspaper account:

N.J. PRISON RIOT
BLAME LAID ON
GOV. DRISCOLL

Responsibility for the current wave of convict rioting in New Jersey State Prisons was laid on the doorstep of Gov. Alfred E. Driscoll today. The governor has consistently ignored charges of gambling, narcotics, home-brew making, special privileges, immorality and other scandalous activities among inmates of Jersey's penal institutions. . . . Gov. Driscoll, flushed with his success at putting Gen. Eisenhower over in the Republican Presidential primary, is spending little time on the prison situation. . . .[5]

For others, however—particularly prison officials—the blame for the riots was to be assigned not to political figures but to the inmates themselves. The disturbance which broke out in 5 Wing on March 29, for example, was largely attributable to the "type of criminal" confined in the cellblock, according to official reports. "Hostile, aggressive, psychopathic, with long records of trouble-making"—so runs the custodians' description—the prisoners in 5 Wing simply needed some chance event to explode into violence. As one guard has said, "To keep those men in there was like trying to hold lions in cages designed for rabbits" and explaining why inmates do not riot is more difficult than explaining why they do.

The committee appointed by the Governor to investigate the insurrections in the penal institutions of New Jersey was more sophisticated, perhaps, in its approach, in that the impersonal forces at work in the prison were given greater recognition. Overcrowding, idleness, heavy turnover in the custodial force, archaic disciplinary practices, inadequacies of the physical plant, heterogeneity of the inmate population, indifferent rehabilitation program, careless work assignments, inadequate salaries for guards, shortage of necessities —all were listed as "basic" causes creating a "feeling of bitterness . . . that was widespread among the prisoners." Any spark might have set it off, notes the committee's report, "by the slow process of spontaneous combustion, or through deliberate lighting of the fuse by the inmate agitators who were determined to set off an explosive demonstration.[6]

The investigating committee's vision of the prison as a powder keg needing only a spark would seem to have two

[5] *Times Herald*, Washington, D.C., Saturday, April 19, 1952.
[6] New Jersey Committee to Examine and Investigate the Prison and Parole Systems of New Jersey, *Report*, November 21, 1952.

points in its favor. First, it avoids the pat explanation of an individual scapegoat. Second, it recognizes that disturbances in the social system we call the prison have their roots in the regime imposed by the custodians on their captives as well as the characteristics of the inmates themselves. *Yet despite its virtues this explanation is unsatisfactory because it fails to give an account of how the prison reaches the point of explosion.* As we have pointed out before, the prison is not always a powder keg, however accurate this term may be to describe the prison in the period immediately preceding a riot. And this fact is clearly recognized by prison officials themselves, in spite of their adherence to what we can call the "powder-keg" theory after riots have occurred. The officials are agreed that there are many points in the prison's history when a serious disturbance is extremely unlikely.[7] By viewing the prison, then, as existing in a constant state of tension or readiness for insurrection, the explanation of the prison's transition to a state of revolt turns on the occurrence of some spark—and this, as we have indicated previously, is apt to be seen as a chance event, an unpredictable element. In short, the "powder-keg" theory of the riots in the prison is, in some ways, worse than no theory at all.

If, however, we take the viewpoint suggested before, namely that our understanding of the riots must rest on an understanding of the larger evolutionary sequence of which they are a part, our attention must be directed not to the "precipitating" events immediately prior to the disturbances but instead to the forces which have molded the New Jersey State Prison in a long-run pattern of social change. And most important among these forces, I think, is the shifting status of what has been called the "semi-official self-government" exercised by the inmate population.[8]

[7] It is true that the report of the investigating committee speaks of unrest in the prison "growing steadily in depth and intensity," thus suggesting that there are times when the prison social system is not ripe for riot. But the report gives no clue as to how or why unrest grows and the idea that the prison is not always ready for a riot but must become so remains simply an implicit suggestion.

[8] See Frank E. Hartung and Maurice Floch, "A Social-Psychological

Now we have discussed the transfer of power from the rulers to the ruled previously, in our analysis of the corruption of the guard's authority as found in the New Jersey State Prison *after* the riots of 1952. The evidence indicates, however, that the transfer of power from officials to inmates was a feature of the prison before the riots as well; and, more importantly, that the extent of what we have chosen to label the corruption of authority was then far greater. In fact, it would appear that in the New Jersey State Prison—as in many other maximum security institutions in the United States—a good deal of the custodian's control had been whittled away over the course of many years. By the late 'Thirties and early 'Forties, the prisoners regulated much of their own affairs. Job assignments and cell assignments, recreational activities and the granting of special "privileges," all had gradually slipped into the hands of the inmate population.

In the middle of the 1940s, however—it is admittedly difficult to date these matters precisely—the officials of the New Jersey State Prison made an effort to reverse the institution's tendency to drift in the direction of ever greater inmate control.[9] The problem was attacked on many fronts and ranged from a severe curtailment of hobby work, which was turning into a disruptive form of "big business" within the walls, to a general tightening of security measures. *And it is this turning point in the administration of the prison which apparently marks the beginning of the tension and unrest that finally flowered in the insurrections of 1952.* As abuses of official rules were curbed, as preferential treatment for favored prisoners was eliminated, as, in short, the social system of the prison was "reformed" in the direction of the free community's image of what a maximum security institution should be like, the New Jersey State Prison moved toward disaster. Thus our glimpse of one portion of the prison's cyclical rhythm punctu-

---

Analysis of Prison Riots: An Hypothesis," *The Journal of Criminal Law, Criminology, and Police Science,* Vol. 47, No. 1, May-June 1956, pp. 51-57.

[9] This attempt to regain power by the officials, like the drift toward corruption, seems to have occurred simultaneously in many other State prisons.

ated by crises reveals a basic paradox: The system breeds rebellions by attempting to enforce the system's rules. The custodians' efforts to secure a greater degree of control result in the destruction of that control, temporary though it may be, in those uprisings we label riots.

This chain of events might, of course, be interpreted as a matter of pushing men nearer and nearer to the breaking point until, under unbearable pressure, prisoners "spontaneously" erupt into demonstrations against their rulers. There is undoubtedly some element of this involved, but it is only a part of the story, for there is another factor of even greater importance which appears to be operative. *The effort of the custodians to "tighten up" the prison undermines the cohesive forces at work in the inmate population and it is these forces which play a critical part in keeping the society of the prison on an even keel.*

Now the occurrence of riots in the prison depends heavily on the emergence of more aggressive, violent, and unstable prisoners into positions of leadership and influence in the society of captives. Dissatisfaction in the inmate population is encouraged and channeled by such men in a spiral of agitation until individual and sporadic impulses to strike back at the captors become fused into an organized plan of insurrection. On the other hand, as long as less aggressive or less alienated prisoners oriented to the theme of inmate cohesion manage to maintain some degree of control over their fellow inmates, the social system of the prison will remain relatively stable. The argot role of the *real man*—the epitome of inmate solidarity—is stressed as the ideal behavior pattern to which all should try to conform. The ability to "take it" rather than the willingness to protest emerges as a dominant value and the "easy bit"—the uneventful period of imprisonment—comes to be recognized as preferable to the violence and disorder of rebellion. And, most importantly, under the sway of such inmate leaders with their commitment to loyalty among prisoners, the sharing of scarce goods, the curbing of hostility and exploitation, and so on, the pains of imprisonment tend

124

to be reduced, thus easing the tensions which lead to riots.[10]

Prisoners oriented to the theme of inmate cohesion can maintain positions of leadership or influence by precept and example, at least in part. As numerous reports on small, informal groups have pointed out, individuals so committed to group solidarity in thought and behavior often rise into positions of dominance by virtue of their personal charisma and are followed because they are admired. But the ability to exercise control or to make one's views carry weight also depends on the use of more material rewards, in the prison as elsewhere. And here we must note that it is the prisoner oriented to the theme of inmate cohesion who is most likely to be favored in the patterns of corruption which grow up between guards and inmates. It is the cohesively-oriented prissoner who "cooperates," who can be "respected" by the officials, and who does not cause "trouble" by exploiting other inmates. He stands opposed to the custodians, it is true, in that he sides with the inmate population in an argument, never betrays a fellow prisoner and derides the values of the law-abiding. But at the same time, his resistance is passive and he does not cause incidents; and, indeed, he can be counted on to point out to other inmates the wisdom of "getting along." Thus it is the cohesively-oriented prisoner who tends to receive the benefits of corruption, the illicit privileges and favors extended by the guards. And it is the distribution of these benefits among other inmates which does much to bolster his influence in the society of captives. An announcement of a supposedly unannounced search for contraband may be given to a favored prisoner who in turn warns a number of favored friends—and thus the unofficial inmate leader acts much like a ward boss dispensing patronage. A desirable job in the officers' messhall, offering a recognized opportunity for gaining extra food, may be awarded the "good" inmate who then

10 If solidarity among inmates increases to too great an extent, of course, the ground may be prepared for organized revolts such as those staged by Conscientious Objectors during the last war. But this is highly unlikely, as we have indicated before.

125

consolidates his standing among other prisoners by means of largesse.

There is always the danger, of course, that the inmate who receives benefits from the custodians will be identified as a *rat* or a *center man* by other prisoners. When a contest for leadership arises, the more aggressive, violent inmates are quick to impugn preferential treatment. The cohesively-oriented prisoner, then, who acts as an inmate leader, must tread a delicate line between rejection of the officials and cooperation. He does so, it appears, by never making explicit bargains with the custodians or acting in a subservient manner. Instead, the favors he receives and passes on are defined by himself and others as his just due and his attempts to curb conflict and disorder are viewed as being for the sake of other inmates rather than for the officials.

In any case, it is the cohesively-oriented prisoner committed to the values of inmate loyalty, generosity, endurance, and the curbing of frictions who does much to maintain the prison's equilibrium. When the custodians strip him of his power —when the custodians destroy the system of illicit privileges, of preferential treatment and laxity which has functioned to increase the influence of the cohesively-oriented prisoner who stands for the value of keeping things quiet—the unstable elements in the inmate population have an opportunity to capitalize on the tensions of prison life and to rise into dominance. The stage has been set for insurrection.[11]

* * * *

As the officials of the New Jersey State Prison are quick to point out, there are disturbances and disturbances and no general explanation is likely to fit them all. Nonetheless, the riots at the Trenton Prison in 1952 are, I think, most explicable in

[11] In some instances it is possible that the officials' attempts to regain control of the prison will drive cohesively-oriented inmates to assume leadership of a rebellion aimed at re-establishing their former favored position. In this sense, some riots may be much like strikes to regain lost benefits. (Cf. Frank E. Hartung and Maurice Floch, *op.cit.*) In general, however, the prison's transitions from stability to instability seem to involve a shift in the elements exercising leadership.

light of the broad theoretical outline sketched in above. The custodial institution cannot long exist at the extreme position of complete and total power lodged in the hands of the official bureaucracy. As we have indicated in an earlier chapter on the defects of total power, the prison suffers from a number of structural flaws which create strong pressures in the direction of what we have chosen to call the corruption of authority, i.e. the imperfect enforcement of the organization's regulations and orders with the tacit acceptance of the officials. The result is a partial transfer of power or control from the captors to the captives, but without such a transfer the accomplishment of the prison's multiple tasks becomes excessively difficult if not impossible. The production goods in the State-Use industries, the performance of institutional housekeeping, the use of facilities directed toward rehabilitation, and the maintenance of internal order are dependent on some degree of uncoerced cooperation; and all must be pursued in addition to the task of preventing escapes. But the corruption of authority has its own dynamic, for corruption seems to breed corruption. The weight of precedent, the present erosive effect of past compromises, the demonstrated ease of administration by concession—all push the social system of the prison deeper and deeper into patterns of compromise between the rulers and the ruled.

The social system of the prison finally reaches a point where the inmates have established their own unofficial version of control. The custodians, in effect, have withdrawn to the walls to concentrate on their most obvious task, the prevention of escapes. The outward guise of the custodians' dominance within the walls is preserved, to be sure, for inmates are still counted, some infractions of the rules are still punished, and prisoners continue to be marched back and forth from their cells. But surveillance has grown lax and guards are careful not to antagonize influential inmates. Institutional supplies are looted with relative ease and goods flow in freely from the outside world. Prisoners administer their own stern justice to inmates who have broken the inmate code and officials seek

127

the advice of their captives with regard to cell and job assignments. The custodial force has achieved what appears to be a peaceful, orderly institution—from the free community's viewpoint—at the cost of abdication in favor of inmate leaders who, no less than the custodians, wish to avoid a public scandal. As we have indicated before, the abdication of the officials is not necessarily a conscious, deliberate affair in the sense that power is transferred to certain inmate leaders on the explicit understanding that they will prevent excessive "trouble" within the walls. But the unofficial control of the prison by the inmates oriented to the theme of inmate cohesion is slipped into more easily because exploitation, conflict among prisoners, and aggression against the custodians is curbed by the inmates themselves. Both the guard *and* the inmate desire an "easy bit" and both want to keep things from being "all shook up."

This illicit form of inmate self-government contains, however, the seeds of its own destruction. Officials may become frightened at the extent to which their own authority has been corrupted, as revealed by an escape attempt gone long undetected due to slack security measures or by a particularly brutal assault of one inmate on another which can be traced to a quarrel over the distribution of contraband. A disgruntled guard, irritated by the power of the inmate "big-shots," may catch the attention of the newspapers, as may a discharged prisoner anxious to settle an old grudge. A conflict within the administrative bureaucracy—a conflict, for example, between those charged with custody and those charged with reformation—may bring the officials' and inmates' modus vivendi into the public view. And there is always the possibility that a change in the political party in office will result in attempts to reform the prison, either as a pretext for the redistribution of political plums or as a sincere commitment to penal progress. In any case, the phase of the prison's cycle in which the inmate population has informally seized much of the power of the captors is far from stable and eventually the custodians will be driven to recapture the institution. And at this point, as I have argued before, the social system of the prison begins its swing toward the moment of explosion. The stabilizing elements in the prison are reduced in effectiveness, tensions mount, and new, aggressive leadership fans the fire of discontent.

IV

Unfortunately this interpretation of prison riots does not allow us to state the length of the different phases in the prison's cycle of social change with any precision nor is the exact process by which one type of leadership among inmates displaces another entirely clear. In the years when this study of the New Jersey State Maximum Security Prison was being undertaken, the institution appeared to be at the beginning of the long slide into patterns of compromise and a recent visit to the prison revealed little change. Information concerning other portions of the cycle was necessarily pieced together from remembrances dimmed by the passage of time and imperfect records. Furthermore, it should be clear that this interpretation of prison riots is greatly over-simplified and that a full account must consider the complicated interrelationships of many factors. Yet even if this interpretation stands in need of a good deal more evidence and development to serve as a theory for prison riots in general and for the insurrections in the Trenton Prison in 1952 in particular, it has the initial, presumptive advantage of analyzing the disturbances in the prison not as isolated, fortuitous events but as an integral part of the nature of confinement. On the one hand, the custodial bureaucracy cannot exert the total power expected by the public and, on the other hand, a small degree of corruption seems impossible to maintain. The public will not tolerate the informal, unofficial control of the institution by the imprisoned criminal and an open breach with the authorities is more intolerable still. I think it is this basic instability of the social system of the prison, under the present terms of confinement, which must be faced by any program which attempts to assess the proper place of the prison in society.

CHAPTER SEVEN

A POSTSCRIPT FOR REFORMERS

"WHILE SOCIETY in the United States gives the example of the most extended liberty, the prisons of the same country offer the spectacle of the most complete despotism," wrote Gustave de Beaumont and Alexis de Tocqueville in their report on American penal institutions in 1833.[1] I think the anomaly must still strike us forcibly today in looking at the prison and it is the nature of this despotic regime in a democratic society which has formed the central concern of our study.

We have seen that keeping men confined is a complex and difficult task, not simply because some men are ingenious in devising ways to escape but also, and more importantly, because the variety of functions which the custodians must perform are often in conflict. Internal order, the organization of prison labor, punishment, and rehabilitation—all must be pursued along with custody within a framework of sharply limited means. The prison officials have attempted to resolve their numerous dilemmas by constructing a vast body of rules and regulations designed to order the activities of the inmate population in minute detail. Such a solution is far from perfect, however, if only on the grounds that the transfer of this intricate and extended control from paper to reality is beset by problems. Unable to depend on a sense of duty among their prisoners as a basis for obedience, barred from the habit-

[1] Gustave de Beaumont and Alexis de Tocqueville, *On the Penitentiary System in the United States and Its Applications in France*, Philadelphia: Carey, Lea, and Blanchard, 1833, p. 47.

130

ual use of force, and lacking an adequate stock of rewards and punishments, the custodians find themselves engaged in a constant struggle to achieve even the semblance of dominance. And the position of the custodial bureaucracy is further undermined by the bonds of friendship which spring up between the guard and his prisoners, by the practices of *quid pro quo* and long familiarity which serve to temper a strict enforcement of the rules.

The fact that the theoretical power of the custodians is imperfect in actuality removes some of the sting of imprisonment as far as the confined criminal is concerned. Yet as much as the power of the custodians may be compromised in the day-to-day routines, the conditions of life posed by imprisonment remain as profoundly disturbing frustrations of the inmate population. Deprived of their liberty, stripped of worldy possessions, denied access to heterosexual relationships, divested of autonomy, and compelled to associate with other deviants, the inmates find that imprisonment still means punishment however much imprisonment may have been softened in this modern era by an accent on humanitarianism and reform. I have suggested that it is these punishing aspects of modern imprisonment, these deprivations or frustrations, which play a crucial part in shaping the inmate social system. It is these deprivations, particularly as they involve a threat or an attack at a deep psychological level, that the inmates must meet and counter. And the inmate population's modes of reactions can be found ranged, I have suggested, between two poles. On the one hand, the prisoner can engage in a highly individualistic war of all against all in which he seeks to mitigate his own plight at the expense of his fellow prisoners; on the other hand, the prisoner can attempt to form a close alliance with his fellow captives and to present a unified front against the custodians. It is the changing mixture of these antithetical behavior patterns and their underlying values which makes up the social system we label so grossly, so overly simply, as the prison community.

131

II

Now we no longer expect the imprisoned criminal to view his cell as "the beautiful gate of the Temple leading to a happy life and by a peaceful end, to Heaven," as did the early prison authorities.[2] But modern society does expect the tyranny of captivity to serve a useful purpose beyond that of keeping known criminals confined, as I have indicated before. The prison, somehow, is expected to turn men from the path of crime to the path of conformity with the law. These expectations concerning the reform of the criminal have in turn given rise to many plans and arguments for reforming the prison. The success or failure of the prison in modifying the inmate's criminality has been deliberately put to one side in our study— our major concern, as I have said, is with the prison as a system of power which is interesting and important in its own right—but I think a few final comments concerning the reform of the prison are in order.

First, it seems clear that criminals will continue to be confined in large groups under conditions of relative deprivation for some time to come, regardless of the consequences. We might attribute this to social inertia, the perhaps still greater economic inertia of investment in existing physical facilities, or a primitive desire for vengeance, but the fact remains. We will not "break down the walls" as some have urged; we will not eliminate these "useless relics of barbarianism"; we will not get rid of the prison whether we think of it as the beautiful gate of the Temple or as that black flower of civilization, as it was described by Hawthorne—at least, not in the short-run future. If criminals confined in prison are not to be dismissed as hopelessly lost from the ranks of the law-abiding, we may try to change the nature of the prison but we will not destroy it. I think a frank recognition of this blunt fact can do much in the formation of an enlightened penal policy.

[2] From the *Thirteenth Annual Report* of the prison inspectors for the Eastern Penitentiary in Philadelphia, quoted in Harry Elmer Barnes and Negley K. Teeters, *New Horizons in Criminology*, New York: Prentice-Hall, Inc., 1952, p. 402.

Second, the prison is an authoritarian community and it will remain an authoritarian community no matter how much the fact of the custodians' power may be eased by a greater concern for the inmates' betterment. Until men willingly forego their freedom and group harmony automatically arises among criminals held captive, the free community will press for institutional controls which will insure custody and the maintenance of order. There are, however, many possible authoritarian communities and some are preferable to others. Insuring custody does not necessarily mean that all escapes must be prevented, for society may decide that some escapes are a price that must be paid if the majority of offenders are to be salvaged. The maintenance of order does not necessarily require that excess of caution which seeks to eliminate the very possibility of any "incident" without regard for the inmate's fearful loss of self-determination, if the free community learns to accept the fact that crime within the walls does not necessarily represent outrageous neglect on the part of the officials. In short, the authoritarian community of the prison does not need to be a harshly repressive one, but the demand for more extensive control than is to be found in society at large will continue and we had best recognize it.

Third, as one writer has wisely pointed out, it is excessively optimistic to expect the prison to rehabilitate 100 percent of its inmates, in light of the fact that it is the more serious or more hardened offender who is most apt to be confined.[3] Plans to increase the therapeutic effectiveness of the custodial institution must be evaluated in terms of the difference between what is done now and what might be done—and the difference may be dishearteningly small. We do not need to assume that man's nature is largely fixed by the adult years nor do we need to condemn efforts to reform the criminal as singularly naïve in order to temper our expectations of success. The greatest naïveté, perhaps, lies in those who believe that because progress in methods for reforming the criminal has

[3] See George B. Vold, "Does the Prison Reform?", *The Annals of the American Academy of Political and Social Science*, Vol. 293, May 1954, pp. 42-50.

been so painfully slow and uncertain in the past, little or no progress can be expected in the future. But by expecting less and demanding less we may achieve more, for a chronically disillusioned public is apt to drift into indifference.

Fourth, present knowledge of human behavior is sufficient to let us say that whatever the influence of imprisonment on the man held captive may be, it will be a product of the patterns of social interaction which the prisoner enters into day after day, year after year, and not of the details of prison architecture, brief exhortations to reform, or sporadic public attacks on the "prison problem." The particular pattern of social interaction into which the inmate enters is, in turn, part of a complex social system with its own norms, values, and methods of control; and any effort to reform the prison—and thus to reform the criminal—which ignores this social system of the prison is as futile as the labors of Sisyphus. The extent to which the existing social system works in the direction of the prisoner's deterioration rather than his rehabilitation; the extent to which the system can be changed; the extent to which we are willing to change it—these are the issues which confront us and not the recalcitrance of the individual inmate.

134

EPILOGUE: THE STRUCTURAL-FUNCTIONAL PERSPECTIVE ON IMPRISONMENT

THE EMERGENCE of a structural-functional perspective on the prison, in the decades immediately following the end of World War II, can be explained in part by the particular interests, personal experiences, and intellectual training of those involved in penology in those years. I believe, however, that the temper of the time—the dominant intellectual fashions, the events in the headlines, the social and political trends of those years—also played a role, providing a spur for a particular kind of theorizing as well as a receptive audience. And pure chance, I think, had an influence as well, in the sense that quite fortuitous events led a number of people—many at the beginning of their academic careers— to immerse themselves in the study of punishment of criminal offenders, bringing a variety of new approaches to the issues. These notes, then, are a form of intellectual history, admittedly impressionistic, anecdotal, personal, and incomplete.

In my own case, for example, I was assigned the criminology course in my first year of teaching as an instructor at Princeton University, although I knew almost nothing about the field, a kind of assignment of little concern apparently to sociology departments then and now. But I began learn-

The material in this epilogue has been reprinted from *Punishment and Social Control*, 2d ed., Blomberg and Cohen, eds., pp. 357–365. Copyright © 2003 Walter de Gruyter, Inc. Published by Aldine de Gruyter, Hawthorne, New York. A collection of essays, *Punishment and Social Control* was published as a tribute to the abiding influence of Sheldon L. Messinger, whose generous insights, suggestions, and criticisms always proved invaluable to his colleagues.

ing what I could, one step ahead (often a misstep) of my students. I was appalled to find that textbooks in the field made almost no effort to examine what I would have thought to be basic issues such as varying conceptions of crime, how and why society defined some behavior criminal, and the meaning of crime from the viewpoint of the offender. The vast body of writing in the law (which I was dimly aware existed) was largely ignored, including the analysis of criminal intent that evidently played a large part in legal thought. And punishment was almost uniformly viewed as a barbarism, and ineffective to boot. A number of liberal sentiments, which I largely shared, seemed to have hardened into a set of clichés that closed off inquiry. But my experience in the army had persuaded me that, for better or for worse, people often became whatever they were assigned regardless of personal proclivities or skills, and I set about becoming a criminologist.

At Princeton in those days many classes were split between lectures and "precepts," or small groups meeting to discuss the lecture material. What was unusual was that the precepts were led not by graduate students but by faculty members, from junior instructors to senior professors. Enrollments in my criminology course began to go up sharply, with the result that the number of necessary precepts increased greatly, requiring more preceptors; and the sociology department persuaded Lloyd McKorkle, the warden of the New Jersey State Maximum Security Prison in the nearby city of Trenton, to meet with one of the discussion groups twice a week.

Lloyd and I became good friends, although I am sure he was more than a little bemused by my naivete and ignorance, and he urged me to make a closer study of the prison. The friendship had two important consequences. For one thing, Lloyd provided me with free and easy access to all parts of the prison, to both guards and inmates, and to the records of the institution. And in frequent, long conversations spread over a number of years, Lloyd and other prison officials provided intimate and detailed accounts of institutional life which proved invaluable.

Donald Cressey tells of a similar chance encounter with another Lloyd—Lloyd Ohlin, in his case—involving a missed connection after a meeting of the American Sociological Association in Urbana, and a shared ride to Chicago, leading to an invitation to study prisons in Wisconsin. Others seem to have had like experiences, in the sense that often seemingly whimsical, random, or accidental events led them into criminology and penology and the establishment of close and prolonged relationships with penal institutions. So much for the idea of an orderly, logical development of an intellectual career. But the important point is that these links with penal institutions produced detailed, intimate knowledge of prison life over a period of years, a knowledge that transcended what could be obtained through questionnaires or interviews, although these too played a part. And the knowledge was different, I think, from that obtained by being an official with an administrative role or being an inmate, although both have made important contributions to the literature of penology.

II

In the first half of this century, interest in the prison had taken six major forms. First, humanitarian concerns centered attention on the brutal and degrading conditions of confinement, and offered various programs of reform. Second, the prison was examined with an eye to the possibilities of rehabilitating the offender, with the deterrent effect of imprisonment largely discounted, as I have noted. Third, a good deal of anecdotal material was offered for public consumption, since tales of life behind bars seemed to feed an endless curiosity about the confinement of dangerous felons. Fourth, linked to this anecdotal material, prisons were periodically subject to exposés detailing mismanagement, graft, and other forms of wrongdoing on the part of officials, with prison scandals serving as a convenient weapon for the party out of power. Fifth, penal institutions served as a topic for historical investigations, although this interest remained limited until the shape of historical inquiries changed and "history from below" became more popular. And finally there was a sociological concern with penal institutions—a concern often marked by a humanitarian impulse and utilitarian considerations of finding more effective means of rehabilitation, but laying claim to scientific objectivity and sociological relevance, and examining such things as patterns of socialization and status.

This sociological work provided an indispensable base for later studies, but with some notable exceptions it was mainly descriptive, an ethnography of the confined. Much of the theorizing centered on the question of "prisonization," or the process by which the individual acquired the values, norms, and attitudes of the inmate subculture, with less attention paid to the question of why the subculture existed in the first place. The diversity of inmate roles was made clear, but their relationship to one another and to the regime of the custodians remained relatively neglected.

After the end of World War II, however, American sociology began to change. Many of the changes were actually a flowering or a development of ideas produced in the 1930s and 1940s, ideas that had simply lain dormant or received little attention in a country preoccupied with war. In any event, research design became much more elaborate and sophisticated, as did the statistical techniques for sample selection and the analysis of data. This push toward quantification was closely linked to the growth of federal funding for the scientific research, with skills in quantification becoming an important qualification for securing funds while at the same time large federal grants provided the resources that made more elaborate quantification possible. "Big time" research was becoming a notable feature of modern sociology. While some substantive areas fell out of fashion, others such as stratification gained increasing attention. And in the area of theory, the ideas of Parsons and Merton, along with those of their disciples, rose into prominence.

Criminology and penology were inevitably influenced to some extent by these developments. As far as the study of the prison was concerned, however, quantitative research with large numbers of respondents and the precise measurement of variables remained relatively rare. The suspicion bordering on paranoia in the prison posed a major problem, since it was extremely difficult and time-consuming to establish the trust necessary for the collection of reliable data by means of questionnaires and interviews, with both guards and inmates. Generally, empirical research on the prison continued to take the form of community studies or participant observation. But a way of looking at the prison, influenced by the ideas of Parsons and Merton, did become much more evident. First, the prison as a whole was taken as the object of study, a small-scale society or social system, with questions about the problems of continuity and order assuming major theoretical significance. Second, the parts of the system—the objectives of the custodial institution, the social and physical environment, the perceptions and social roles of guards and inmates, and so on— were seen as interrelated elements to be analyzed for their impact on one another and the system as a whole. Emphasis was placed not simply on the intended consequences of rules and behavior but on the unintended or latent outcomes as well. Third, the prison was seen as providing an opportunity for "middle-range" theorizing, with the special conditions of custodial institutions setting definite limits on generalization but offering the possibility of greater insights on the nature of totalitarian control. And fourth— and perhaps most important—the norms of both guards and inmates were seen as being significantly shaped by the system of power in which they played out their social roles. The existence of norms was not to be taken as a given, with commitment to those norms seen as a matter of socialization, enculturation, the transmission of culture, learning theory, differential association, and so on. Instead, the existence of norms was a problem to be solved, and the task was to analyze norms as a function of the social structure or social system in which individuals found themselves.

These themes were not original nor were they unique to the study of the prison. Albert Cohen, for example, in his book *Delinquent Boys* (1955), had set forth a clear and powerful argument for the need to explore the origins of subcultures rather than merely to study the process of their acquisition, and had traced his ideas to Pitirim Sorokin's concern with the rise and fall of total systems.[1] But the combination of these themes, the emphasis given to them, and the primary interest in the prison itself rather than the effectiveness of the prison for rehabilitation, deterrence, or retribution all brought something different to penology.

Two other things were important, I think, in the development of a changed perspective on imprisonment. First, there were some forty riots in eighteen months in American prisons, beginning in the early part of 1952. Prisons, obviously, were not working very well, and public concern with the issue encouraged an academic interest. Thus, for example, funds were provided by the Social Science Research Council for a series of meetings, in 1956 and 1957, for a group of social scientists working in this area, leading to the publication in 1960 of *Theoretical Studies in the Social Organization of the Prison*.[2] Second, the 1950s saw an increased interest in systems of total power as more and more information about Nazi concentration camps became available. This factor acted in a very indirect fashion, I believe, and the analysis of concentration camps never became a part of American criminology in any full or systematic way. Nevertheless, reports on concentration camps became an important part of the intellectual climate, particularly

[1] Albert K. Cohen, *Delinquent Boys*, New York: Free Press, 1955.
[2] Richard Cloward, ed., *Theoretical Studies in the Social Organization of the Prison*, New York: Social Science Research Council, 1960.

through Bruno Bettelheim's "Individual and Mass Behavior in Extreme Situations" in the early 1940s, and books such as Eugen Kogon's *The Theory and Practice of Hell* in the 1950s, and Hannah Arendt's *Eichmann in Jerusalem* in the 1960s.[3]

III

The structural-functional approach to the prison rarely concerned itself with precise definitions, conceptual elaboration, or the logical analysis of causal chains—or, indeed, the accumulation of a large mass of empirical data. Instead, I think its claim to attention rested on a set of basic insights that found a sympathetic audience:

1. It was recognized that prison, like any other complex social system persisting through time, could not be run by the use of force alone, that some degree of voluntary cooperation on the part of those who were ruled was necessary. The problem then was how this cooperation could be obtained.

2. The rewards and punishments legally available to the prison authorities were generally inadequate, as far as securing cooperation was concerned. Furthermore, the task of running the prison and securing cooperation was severely hampered by the fact that the prison was assigned objectives that were often contradictory or in conflict with one another. Thus, for example, efforts to rehabilitate inmates were frequently undone by the requirements of maintaining security and preventing disorder.

3. Some degree of cooperation could be obtained—and usually was—by a system of illegal or forbidden rewards, such as guards ignoring the infraction of prison rules by inmates. Prisoners were allowed to engage in various forms of deviant behavior—ostensibly of a minor sort—in exchange

---

[3] Bruno Bettelheim, "Individual and Mass Behavior in Extreme Situations," *Journal of Abnormal and Social Psychology*, Vol. 38, 1943, pp. 447–451; Eugen Kogon, *The Theory and Practice of Hell*, New York: Farrar, Straus, 1950; Hannah Arendt, *Eichmann in Jerusalem: A Report on the Banality of Evil*, New York: Viking, 1963.

for a quiet institution. This pattern of the custodians breaking the rules for the sake of peace and quiet was part of an extensive pattern of "corruption" based on friendship and the innocuous encroachment on the guards' duties on the part of inmates.

4. Imprisonment involved a set of deprivations that went far beyond the loss of liberty or material comfort. Prisoners were faced with a number of psychological threats to their self-conception or sense of worth, such as being reduced to childhood's dependence or being forced into homosexual liaisons.

5. Much of the behavior of inmates could be interpreted or understood as attempts, conscious or unconscious, to meet and counter the problems posed by the deprivations of prison life, including the potent threats to the ego. In later years, critics such as John Irwin would claim that the behavior patterns of inmates were rooted in a thieves' subculture, and much was made of an indigenous versus an imported model of the inmate social system.[4] From the structural-functional perspective, however, the important issue was how the behavior of inmates was related to their present predicament rather than the possible influence of life before confinement. And although inmates' behavior was probably conditioned by prior criminal patterns, the crucial issue was how these general tendencies—such as the vaunted loyalty among thieves or the instrumental use of violence—might be reinforced or called into play by the realities of prison life. (I think there was a common feeling that the inmate social system seen in prisons at the time would very likely come into existence almost without regard to inmates' criminal histories. I suppose this idea was based at least in part on assumptions about the power of totalitarian systems to shape behavior and the limited possibilities of dealing with the threats posed by imprisonment.)

6. It was claimed that the behavior patterns of inmates

---

[4] John Irwin, *The Felon*, Englewood Cliffs, NJ: Prentice-Hall, 1970.

142

sprang from a set of values, attitudes, and beliefs that found expression in the so-called inmate code couched in prison argot. This code held forth a pattern of approved conduct, but as Shelly Messinger and I tried to make clear, it was an ideal rather than a description of how inmates behaved. It was argued that an important theoretical and empirical variable was to be found in the extent to which inmates actually did or did not conform to the inmate code with its demands for inmate solidarity, and this variation was likely to be a vital factor in determining the extent to which rehabilitation was possible in a prison setting.

These ideas came to be labeled "the structural-functional perspective on the prison," and I suppose that designation was appropriate, in the sense that interest in the prison centered on (1) the social structure of the prison as a whole; and (2) the ways in which beliefs, norms, and behavior of both inmates and guards functioned to maintain the prison as an ongoing system. The astonishing thing about prisons, from this viewpoint, was the fact that they did not degenerate into perpetual chaos on the one hand, or on the other, into the frozen order of masses of men locked in solitary confinement. Somehow, a social system, involving complex interaction, was kept going. It was precisely this fact, I think, that Shelly and I concentrated on in our discussion of the inmate beliefs and norms that we saw, not as an extension of the outlaw's code—a somewhat romantic notion, perhaps—but as an understandable response to the rigors of confinement, specifically addressed to the problems of prison life.

IV

As I look back on the development of these ideas, some forty years after the fact, I still think they were a worthwhile innovation despite their limitations. Obviously, the nature of imprisonment has changed in a number of ways, such as the greatly increased balkanization of the inmate population along racial and ethnic lines described by James Jacobs,[5] court intervention in the legal powers of the custodians, and shifts in the composition of the inmate population, and these changes must modify our view of the social system of the custodial institution. The neglect of race relations in the prisons in the 1950s is rather striking, and I think this was probably due to two things. First, the sociologists writing about the prison were almost exclusively white, and I suspect this helped to shape not only the range of their concerns but also their ability to establish relationships of trust with black inmates. And second, there was an assumption that the social systems of black and white inmates—and their relationships with the power structure of the prison— were essentially the same. Along with this it was assumed that blacks and whites in prison frequently achieved a kind of modus vivendi and, indeed, that the solidarity of inmates would, to some extent, override the antagonisms of race.

All this changed, of course, in the ensuing decades, and group conflict rather than inmate solidarity became a paramount feature of many custodial institutions. Not only did blacks and whites often move to violent confrontations, but bikers, different factions of Hispanics, political radicals, and others formed contesting alliances. Nonetheless, I believe the structural-functional perspective continues to provide a valid picture of the broad outlines of the nature of imprisonment in America today, with the recognition that inmate solidarity has fractured, in many institutions, along a variety of fault lines.

However, I must admit I am also struck by the fact that academic studies of the prison seem to have had little impact on public policy. A good deal of the research on prisons has been linked to the hope that society can build a more humane and more effective system of criminal justice, with a decreased reliance on punishment; what has happened, in

[5] James B. Jacobs, *New Perspectives on Prisons and Imprisonment*, Ithaca, NY: Cornell University Press, 1983.

fact, in the last twenty-five years or so, is that the philosophy of "lock 'em up and throw away the key" has gained ground in the United States rather than being diminished. Rates of imprisonment have increased sharply.[6] Public support for parole has gone down, and programs of treatment within prisons have been eliminated or reduced. Harsher sentences have become more popular, as in the case of the so-called war on drugs, but with little apparent effect on crime rates.

It is possible, of course, that the problems of the prison are beyond the reach of the social engineering often envisioned by social sciences—and it must be admitted that the social sciences have unquestionably suffered from an amazing hubris as far as their power to change social reality is concerned. It is also possible that more punitive public policies of recent years might be seen as a misguided but sincere effort to come to grips with changing circumstances, such as high crime rates, or as an acceptance of empirical research claiming nothing much works when it comes to treatment without prison walls. I suspect, however, that the increased strength of the punitive viewpoint is only marginally related to increases in crime rates or an objective analysis of the outcome of efforts at reformation. In my opinion, when all is said and done about rehabilitation, incapacitation, and deterrence, the prison continues to be seen primarily as a flawed but essential instrument of retribution, as far as the great majority of the public is concerned. Stories of crime and punishment have an ancient lineage and exercise a perennial appeal, and it is undoubtedly true that our ideas about how to handle the criminal are likely to be shaped by the entertainments of the mass media and the emotional rhetoric of political speeches. But it is also probably true that our ideas about punishment are

[6] For a comprehensive review of what is commonly referred to as mass imprisonment in the United States, see David Garland, ed., "Special Issue on Mass Imprisonment in the USA," *Punishment & Society*, Vol. 3, No. 1, 2001, pp. 5–199.

shaped as well by deep-seated cultural dictates and persistent personal inclinations. Sociology has been inclined to dismiss the demand for punishment largely as an irrelevant barbarism or as the expression of fluctuations in the political climate. If we are to achieve a better, more complex understanding of the forces that shape punishment in general or imprisonment in particular, I think we will need to work out a more profound analysis of the public's view of punishment, and to examine it as a moral choice filled with the ambiguities, uncertainties, prejudices, and efforts to be rational that shape so much of human behavior.

146

APPENDIX A:

A NOTE ON METHOD

THE data for this study were gathered from a variety of sources, the most important of which were as follows: a) official publications and reports of the Department of Institutions and Agencies for the State of New Jersey; b) regulations, standard operating procedures, monthly reports, and similar material issued by the Trenton Prison; c) individual files for the members of the inmate population, containing a case history for each prisoner; d) tape-recorded interviews with inmates; e) questionnaires; concerning the behavior of a random sample of 200 prisoners—both in terms of inmate with inmate and inmate with guard—the information being supplied by each prisoner's Wing guard and Shop officer; f) personal observation; and g) informal interviews with senior officials, guards, and inmates.

I think the last source of material—the relatively "unstructured" talks with the captors and their captives—was the most useful by far, despite the dangers introduced by a lack of standardization and undoubted biases of selection. Of particular worth were the many, long discussions with the Warden, Dr. Lloyd W. McCorkle, who was as much a student of the prison as its chief administrator. In addition, I found it possible to establish fairly close rapport with some twenty inmates of varied backgrounds and patterns of reactions to confinement; and these men served in effect as a panel which could be interviewed again and again over the course of time.

There are, I believe, two serious methodological difficulties in studying an organization such as the prison, aside from the obvious difficulty of establishing close relationships—so necessary for interviews of any depth—with a large number of randomly selected, and inevitably suspicious, inmates. First, the observer is constantly in peril of being "conned" by highly articulate, glib prisoners who seek some personal advantage. Such inmates are quite ready to talk—in fact, they are far too ready—and the observer must make

147

a great effort to shake them loose and to get at their more reticent, inarticulate fellow captives. Second, in the polarized society of the prison it is extremely difficult not to become partisan, consciously or unconsciously. I believe, however, that it is only by remaining firmly neutral in one's sympathies that a valid picture of prison life can be uncovered. It is for this reason that "participant observation"—either as a guard or as an inmate—is apt to prove defective as a technique for securing data, although it undoubtedly leads to a far more detailed view of *either* the captives *or* the captors than is possible by other means. The realities of imprisonment are, however, multi-faceted; there is not a single true interpretation but many, and the meaning of any situation is always a complex of several, often conflicting viewpoints. This fact can actually be an aid to research concerning the prison rather than a hindrance, for it is by the simultaneous consideration of divergent viewpoints that one begins to see the significant aspects of the prison's social structure. One learns not to look for the one, true version; instead, one becomes attuned to contradiction. And it is only by remaining neutral that one can go from captives to captors, from captors to captives, to hear the conflicting stories. This matter of circulating in a social system to record an event from many different vantage points may not warrant the dignity of labelling it a method of research, but it proved to be the key to the society of captives.

APPENDIX B:

THE ROUTINE OF IMPRISONMENT

THE details of existence in the institution vary slightly depending on the day of the week, the season of the year, and the particular cellblock or Wing which is being· described. Nonetheless, the routine of one Wing—or one day—can pretty well stand for all. The following chronicle, written by the officials of the New Jersey State Prison and filed as part of their standard operating procedures, lists the sequence of duties for the guard assigned to 2 Left;[1] and with its account of bells and inspections, of reports and continual tallies, this detailed scrutiny of the guard at work conveys the flavor of imprisonment as little else can.

FIRST SHIFT

6:15 A.M.
Pick up Wing Keys and Pass Books at the Grill Gate.

6:20 A.M.
Line up for Roll Call and Inspection in Center.

6:22 A.M.
Proceed to 2 Left and relieve third shift officer.
Take written physical count of Wing, making sure all inmates are present, alive, and well. Check your actual count with the Roster Board and, if it corresponds with your physical count, make up and sign Daily Wing Count Slip and send same to Center. If Roster Board and your physical count do not correspond, take the count again. If it still disagrees, send your actual physical count to Center and notify Center of the difference in the two figures.
After the Bell from Center certifying that a proper count has

---

[1] Each Wing in the prison is given a number and the two banks of cells in each Wing are designated as the left and the right section. Thus guards and inmates speak of 1 left and 1 right, 2 left and 2 right, etc.

been made of the entire institution you may let your Head Runner out of cell. The Head Runner will let out the other tier runners. The runners are to assume posts on their respective tiers to open or close brakes only upon orders from Officer. Unlock balance of brakes and cell doors, keeping brakes on and leaving cell doors closed with straps free so that men may open cell doors when brakes are released.

Runners will then proceed along their tiers calling out DOCTOR CALL. They will take down the first and last name, number and cell location of men who wish to see the doctor. Make up Doctor Call Slips and Shop Excuse Slips for these men. The officer will inspect and sign these slips and they will be picked up by the Hospital Runner.

6:30 A.M.

Open one tier at a time to allow men to sweep dirt out of cells, to be put into tier dirt box drawn by runner for this purpose, and put laundry out on Laundry Day. Any runner you designate may act as Laundry Man. He has a Wing Record Book and checks out each item with Laundry Runners, and when the laundry is returned he will check all garments to make certain none are missing.

Take a count of sheets and pillow cases going out of the Wing to the laundry; and, on return, check inmate number on each item as well as total count.

The officer will arrange all items with the help of the tier and Head Runner, marking cell location in chalk on each item and giving same to proper tier runners for distribution.

6:35 A.M.

The Wing Officer will receive notice from the Center (by phone) to send the Tag Shop and Outside Shop men to Mess. This is a continuous Mess and, subsequently, the officer will receive notice (by bells) to send the other inmates to Mess. Check all cells for irregularities.

As soon as men return from the Mess Hall they should go to their cells and enter immediately. No loitering or out of place is to be permitted.

Wing is to be kept quiet and orderly at all times. While men are at Mess, check tiers and cells for irregularities.

It is a practice to alternate the two tiers that go first to Mess.

7:30 A.M.

Tag Shop men leave Wing for Shop upon call from Center.

7:50 A.M.

Outside Shop men leave Wing for shops upon call from Center.

8:10 A.M.

All men should be back in Wing from Mess Hall.

SUNDAY AND HOLY DAYS—Roman Catholic Mass

8:15 A.M.

Inside Shop men leave Wing for shops by bells from Center. Machine, Shoe, Tailor, Print, Repair, School.

Doctor Call. Thursday is Prescription Day. After Doctor Call, inmates return to their cells. Those inmates who are to report to the Hospital for a further check by the Doctor are detained in the Wing until called for by an escorting officer.

SATURDAY AND HOLIDAYS—Yard Out

8:20 A.M.

2 Right Officer escort inmates from 2 Right and 2 Left to Yard Dump with Wing trash. Inspect trash when it is dumped for contraband and evidence of escape attempt or irregularities.

While 2 Right Officer is escorting inmates to Yard Dump, 2 Left Officer locks all remaining inmates on both sides in their cells.

8:25 A.M.

Band men leave Wing, on call from Center.

8:30 A.M.

Check inmates to determine if all those who are supposed to be in Wing are actually present. Check all cells, tiers, bars, ceilings, and floors. Search cells. Do clerical work whenever time is available.

9:00 A.M.

Sunday—Protestant Church Service

9:30 A.M.

2 Left Officer will relieve 2 Right Officer to go to Mess. Return to Wing by 10:00 A.M.

10:00 A.M.

2 Right Officer will relieve 2 Left Officer to go to Mess. Return to Wing by 10:30 A.M.

10:30 A.M.

Idle men go to Mess. They should all return to Wing by 11:10 A.M.

11:25 A.M.

Outside Shop men return to Wing.

11:35 A.M.

Inside Shop men return to Wing.

11:40 A.M.

Take physical count of Wing and, upon finding correct, fill out and sign Daily Wing Count Slip and send same to Center by Head Runner.

11:50 A.M.

Tag Shop and Outside Shop men are called to Mess from Center by phone. Laundry men may also be called to Mess at this time.

12:00 NOON

Inside Shop men go to Mess—by bell from Center.

12:30 P.M.

Tag Shop and Outside Shop men return to work on call from respective Shop Officers.

12:45 P.M.

All men back in Wing from Mess.

SUNDAY—Bible Class

12:55 P.M.

Inside Shop men return to work on bell from Center.

1:05 P.M.

Idle men to Yard, Corridor or Movies on bell from Center— as scheduled and unless restricted. Check to determine if those men under restriction have not gone out to Yard, etc. Escort men to Yard and return to Wing.

1:20 P.M.

Lock all remaining inmates in their cells. Take count of men staying in their cells. Make out a count sheet of men in the Wing, and Wing total count, for the 2:20 P.M. Officer. Make out Census Sheet and take same to Center before 2:00 P.M.

152

Inspect floors of cells on Flats, check tiers, all cells, bars, doors, cell ceilings on top tiers, for security, cleanliness; issue passes, etc. Make out Special Reports of Security. Check cells at any time during the day whenever there are no movements and time is available. The regular assigned Day Wing Officer requisitions clothing, household and other necessary items needed to take care of the men and operate the Wing.

SECOND SHIFT

2:20 P.M.

Line up for Roll Call and Inspection in Center.

2:25 P.M.

Proceed to Wing and relieve 6:20-2:20 Officer. Take physical count of all inmates in cells. Report total count to Center by phone, saying, viz.: Wing 2 Left—24 in, total 98.

The difference between the 24 and 98 may be broken down into various categories: Yard, work, Choir, passes, etc.

The total of these added together should correspond with the total Wing Count. If any man from these groups returns to the Wing they should go to their cells and be locked in.

2:30 P.M.

Unlock cell doors of Wings 2 Right and 2 Left, leaving brakes on so that the men cannot open doors.

3:00 P.M.

Inmates return from Yard—or Corridor—and are locked in.

3:15 P.M.

Repair Shop men return from work.

3:20 P.M.

Outside Shop men return from work.

3:30 P.M.

Inside Shop men return from work.

3:45 P.M.

Take full count and report to Center by phone.

3:50 P.M.

Men leave Wing for Second Yard Period by Bell from Center.

153

3:55 P.M.

Check cells and tiers for irregularities. If there are any men from the Outside Details returning from work they are to be locked in their cells or go to the yard.

4:30 P.M.

Officer has supper served him in the Wing.

4:45 P.M.

Let Cook House men out of their cells to go to work. Give out medicine.

5:45 P.M.

Men return from Second Yard period. Secure Wing and take full count. Report count to Center by phone—listing name, number, cell location and shop assignment of any men missing from count. From now until Mess Bell sounds—permit men to take showers, two at a time. This may not be possible with late yard. Hang over from early yard must bathe in cells.

6:00 P.M.

Men leave for Mess Hall for evening meal on Bell from Center. Buckets should be brought down at this time to be filled. Men returning from mess pick up buckets and go direct to their cells. As soon as all men return to the Wing, take a written physical count. Check your actual count with the Roster Board and, if it corresponds with your physical count, make up and sign Daily Wing Count Slip and send same to Center.

If Roster Board and your physical count do not correspond, take the count again. If it still disagrees, send your actual physical count to the Center and notify Center of the difference in the two figures. If men should be missing from the Wing on Special Detail, passes, etc., record same on count slip and notify the Center. After the notification from Center certifying that a proper count has been made of the entire institution, the evening recreational program begins. When an evening move, such as TV takes place, check to determine how many attend and check on double-ups. Report TV attendance count to Center. Lock remaining inmates in their cells.

7:00 P.M.

Give out packages and mail.

7:50 P.M.

(Summer Schedule) Start ringing Center Bell ten minutes of the hour to the hour, and twenty minutes after the hour to the half-hour. During the Winter schedule start ringing bell at 6:50 P.M. Change direction—skip tiers—alternate time.

7:30 P.M.

Wing, cell and institutional transfers are made at this time. Patrol tiers, and attend sick calls at all times. Lock up Cook House men on 2 Right.

9:30 P.M.

Men return from TV or other evening movements. Lock men in their cells, secure Wing and take Check Count of entire Wing. This is the last movement until relieved.

THIRD SHIFT

10:20 P.M.

Line up in Center for Roll Call and Inspection. Proceed to Wing and take actual physical count of all inmates in Wing, making certain that all are present, alive, and well. Beware of dummies.

Check your actual count with the Roster Board and, if it corresponds with your physical count, make out and sign Daily Wing Count Slip and give same to Officer you are relieving. This officer should remain in the Wing until you have completed your count. If Roster Board and your physical count do not correspond, take the count again. If it still disagrees, notify Center and await further orders. While waiting, both officers should investigate the situation. If the count is correct allow relieved Officer to proceed to Center with your signed count slip. Read all notices and orders on bulletin board and elsewhere in the Wing.

Start ringing Center Bell every half-hour on both sides of the Wing—five minutes to the hour and twenty minutes after the hour.

10:55 P.M.

Ring Center Bell. Make round of Wing (change direction). (Change time per location.)

11:25 P.M.

Ring Center Bell. Make round of Wing.

11:35 P.M.

Bakery inmates are unlocked and escorted to Bake Shop by Bakery Officer and Wing Officer.

155

11:55 P.M.

Ring Center Bell. Make round of Wing (alternate time). Repeat the same procedure the rest of the tour, checking for sick calls or other irregularities until 5:30 A.M.

5:30 A.M.

Officer from the Center will report to assist you in getting Cook House men out to work. He will bring keys from Center with him. When Cook House men are all out, lock cell doors, brakes, and Wing doors. Keys are returned to Center by assisting Officer.

5:55 A.M.

Ring Center and check Wing. Stand by for 6:20 Relief Officer. Make out special reports and Observation Reports.

INDEX

African Americans, ix, xxi–xxii. *See also* prisons, race relations in
Anderson, Elijah, xxiii
Arendt, Hannah, 141
Arnold, Thurmond, 38

ball busters, xii, 99–102, 100–101n16, 103
Beaumont, Gustave de, 130
Bennett, James V., 14
Bettelheim, Bruno, 75–76, 141
boot camps, xix
brainwashing, 12n
Braman, Donald, xxi
bureaucratic indifference, principle of, 74–75

center men, xii, 89–90, 94
Charge Slips, 56; samples of, 43–45
cigarettes, as a medium of prisoner exchange, 94n
Clemmer, Donald, xv
"coercive compliance structure," xvii
Cohen, Albert, 140
Cohen, Morris, 11
Colvin, Mark, xvii
concentration camps, 140–41
Cressey, Donald, 137
criminal behavior, 38
criminals, alienation of from society, 66–67
criminology, 139
custodians, 13–14, 19, 21, 22, 25;

control mechanisms of, 33; number of, 40; power of, 37, 37n, 41–42, 46–48. *See also* custodians, bureaucracy of; guards
custodians, bureaucracy of, 41–42, 74n, 128, 130–31; coercive practices used by, 48–52; lower-ranking guards as essential to, 52–54; structural defects of, 61–62; undermining of bureaucratic power, 42–43, 46–48, 123
custody. *See* incarceration

Davis, Kingsley, 6
Delinquent Boys (A. Cohen), 140
DiIulio, John, xvi–xvii
Driscoll, Alfred E., 22, 120–21
Duneier, Mitchell, xxiii
Durkheim, Emile, 38

East, Norwood, 94n
Eichmann in Jerusalem (Arendt), 141
Enlightenment, the, xxix
escape artists, 22, 80, 80n

fags, 95–99; and the punks/fags distinction, 96–97
Feeley, Malcolm, xix
Felon, The (Irwin), xv–xvi
fish, 94
Fleisher, Mark, xix–xx
fortitude, 101–2
Frankel, Emil, 6–7

157